ISLAM EXPLAINED

Essential reading for anyone
who wants to know more about Islam

SHAIK KADIR

Marshall Cavendish
Editions

© 2017 Marshall Cavendish International (Asia) Private Limited

First published 2006. This edition updated and revised 2017.

Published by Marshall Cavendish Editions
An imprint of Marshall Cavendish International

A member of the
Times Publishing Group

The publisher makes no representation or warranties with respect to the contents of this book, and specifically disclaims any implied warranties or merchantability or fitness for any particular purpose, and shall in no event be liable for any loss of profit or any other commercial damage, including but not limited to special, incidental, consequential, or other damages.

Other Marshall Cavendish Offices:
Marshall Cavendish Corporation. 99 White Plains Road, Tarrytown NY 10591-9001, USA • Marshall Cavendish International (Thailand) Co Ltd. 253 Asoke, 12th Flr, Sukhumvit 21 Road, Klongtoey Nua, Wattana, Bangkok 10110, Thailand • Marshall Cavendish (Malaysia) Sdn Bhd, Times Subang, Lot 46, Subang Hi-Tech Industrial Park, Batu Tiga, 40000 Shah Alam, Selangor Darul Ehsan, Malaysia

Marshall Cavendish is a registered trademark of Times Publishing Limited

National Library Board, Singapore Cataloguing in Publication Data

Names: Shaik Kadir.
Title: Islam explained : essential reading for anyone who wants to know more about Islam / Shaik Kadir.
Description: Second edition. I Singapore : Marshall Cavendish Editions, [2017]
Identifiers: OCN 989867971 I 978-981-4779-73-9 (paperback)
Subjects: LCSH: Islam. I Islamic ethics. I Islam--Customs and practices.
Classification: DDC 297--dc23

Printed in Singapore by Markono Print Media Pte Ltd

CONTENTS

♦ INTRODUCTION

Islam expanded rapidly within the lifetime of Prophet Muhammad. The religion has travelled far and wide and continues to spread fast.

Today, one in five people in the world is a follower of the Islamic faith. Islam embraces the lives of various races and cultures across the globe, including the USA and Europe. This happens because of the religion's concept, teachings, rationality and beauty. Unfortunately, misinformed people might blame Islam for the indulgence of some misled Muslims, often as lone wolf, in violence and terrorism, ignoring the Qur'anic instruction: "Do no evil nor mischief on the (face of the) earth." (2:60). But, the vast majority of people, even if they do not know about Islam, will not blame Islam for the wrongdoings of the small number of evil-doers as they recognise that all religions teach righteousness.

The Islamic religion provides comprehensive guidance in spiritual and social matters, with rules and regulations on everyday issues such as hygiene, diet, education, work, the roles of men and women, and positive work attitude.

Islam teaches its adherents to live a balanced life between seeking the bounties of this world and preparing for the bliss of the Hereafter. Islam does not preach terrorism, violence or any other obnoxious acts. On the contrary, the Qur'an says: "Who is better in speech than one who calls (mankind) to God, work righteousness, and says 'I am of those who bow in Islam.'" (41:33) This verse informs the Muslim that he ought to observe the following three main obligations:

- To call people to God — that is, to call people to the Divine Path of Righteousness.
- To work righteousness — that is, to carry out righteous deeds and actions.

- To bow to Islam — that is, to completely follow the teachings of Islam.

There can be no greater or so sublime a duty than to undertake these three noble obligations in bringing and sustaining goodness, truth and beauty on earth. Indeed, undertaking such responsibilities would be the source of the Muslim's honour, pride and dignity.

Islam is not responsible for those Muslims involved in terrorism and violence, who completely ignored, or were unaware of, the clear-cut Qur'anic command that if anyone kills an innocent person (Muslim or non-Muslim), it would be as if he had killed the whole mankind (5:32) for which the sin is enormous. However, these misguided Muslims make up only a tiny fraction of the vast majority of practising Muslims who adhere to Islam and find peace and happiness in it. People should know what Islam really is. They should explore Islam to discover its truth as can be seen from its concept — that Islam which started with moral teachings by the first man (Prophet Adam), developed with the advancement of human needs by succeeding prophets, like Prophet Abraham, Prophet Moses and Prophet Jesus (or Jesus Christ), and finally completed at the time of, and by, Prophet Muhammad. This concept is like the education system, from primary school level to tertiary level — the higher the level, the more rewarding is the magnitude because of its comprehensiveness, though each level has its own merit for spiritual enlightenment.

This book would certainly meet the demand of such a seeker of knowledge by providing him an insight into this beautiful, rational, dynamic and forward-looking religion.

When exploring Islam, it is vital to look at Islam from a total approach — from its concept to its moral and practical teachings. It is to provide an explanation of the foundation and substance of Islam that this book has been written very simply and concisely in topical form with numerous supporting quotations from the Qur'an (Words of God) and the Hadith (sayings and deeds of the Prophet).

Indeed no one book is able to provide answers to all the imaginable questions or to thoroughly satisfy every seeker of knowledge. This book is no different. Anyone requiring an in-depth knowledge on any aspect of Islam may consult relevant books written in English by Muslim academics and scholars, and even approach local Muslim organisations for advice.

Finally, this handy book is dedicated to anyone and everyone, irrespective of race, religion or culture, who reads it to know and understand Islam and Muslims better so that together we can live harmoniously, respecting one another, and working towards making the world a better place to live in.

Shaik Kadir
July 2017

🕌 INITIAL NOTES

Some explanation is required for the way certain words, spelling and expressions are used in this book.

Special terms
All special Islamic terms are written in italics and their interpretation is given immediately within brackets, like *"khutbah* (sermon)"*, instead of placing the words and their interpretation in a separate glossary at the end of the book.

The term *"solat* (Islamic prayers)" is used instead of the term "prayers" because *"solat"* is a very special and formalised activity totally different from "prayer".

Salutation for prophets
When the name of Prophet Muhammad is mentioned, Muslims say *"Sallallah alaihi wasallam"* which means "Peace be upon him", often abbreviated to PBUH in Islamic literature. This is a salutation made as a mark of respect and love for Prophet Muhammad as well as all the prophets of Islam. In this book, the salutation is omitted. Muslim readers are free to make the salutation as and when they come across the names of the prophets.

Voice of God
The voice in the Qur'an (which is in Arabic) is always God's. In the Qur'an, God speaks directly to Prophet Muhammad, Muslims, believers or mankind. At times, God refers to Himself as "God" ("Allah") and "He"; sometimes as "I", and at other times as "We", depending on the aura, tone and situation of the speech He makes. In the Arabic language, "We" is used in the singular sense by authorities as a mark

of politeness, hence "We" is not indicative of a plural pronoun. God is one and only in Islam.

Direct speeches

The expression "God says: ..." is used when quoting from the Qur'an. This approach is used because the entire Qur'an contains God's Words. However, only words and verses in the original language, Arabic, are God's Words. Those in any language, including English, are merely interpretations, as translation from the original to any other language is impossible to be rendered with exact meaning.

Sometimes instead of the phrase "God says: ...", the phrase "The Qur'an says: ..." is used. As the whole of the Qur'an contains God's Words, both phrases mean the same.

References

Every chapter of the Qur'an has a name. For example, Chapter 7 of the Qur'an is called "Al-A'raf" (The Heights) but in this book, the name of the chapter is omitted; instead the chapter number and the verse number are given in brackets. The chapter number is mentioned first. An example is verse 38, taken from Chapter 30 which is called "Ar-Rum" (The Roman Empire). The verse is quoted thus: "God says: 'Give what is due to kindred, the needy and the wayfarer. That is best for those who seek God, and it is they who will prosper." (30:38) (See Appendix A for the names of all the chapters of the Qur'an and their respective interpretation in English.)

Readers may sometimes find the same Qur'anic references given at different places of the book but the verses quoted look different. This is not a typo error, but because the actual verse in the Qur'an is a long verse a part of it is quoted in one section to support certain narration and another part of the verse is quoted elsewhere to support another subject.

The Hadith

The Words of God are contained in the Qur'an, while the words of Prophet Muhammad are contained in the Hadith. Like the quotations from the Qur'an, those from the Hadith have their references. The references are omitted in this book as they are usually lengthy. Instead, the expression "The Prophet said: ..." is used when quoting from the Hadith. This is a common practice of many Muslim writers.

Malay spelling
Certain words, like "*Insha-Allah*" (God willing), "*Ishak*" (the fifth and last prayer of the day) and "Shawal" (the tenth month of the Muslim calendar) have not been spelt "*Insya-Allah*", "*Isyak*" and "Syawal" respectively according to the official Romanised Malay spelling. This is because readers from countries outside Singapore and Malaysia may find it difficult to pronounce these words when they are spelt with "sy" for "sh".

1 ⚊ INTELLIGENT BEINGS

God, in His plan, created three kinds of intelligent beings — angels, Satan and humankind — each with specific nature and characteristics. God created the angels and Satan without the endowment of choice. Angels and Satan do not eat, drink or sleep and are neither male nor female. They are invisible to human beings. God then created human beings (represented by Adam and Eve) who were endowed with choice. As such, God sent prophets from time to time to guide them.

ANGELS AND SATAN
The nature and characteristics of angels and Satan are different from those of human beings.

Angels
Angels have been created solely to obey God in performing certain spiritual responsibilities. The Qur'an says: "They do not disobey God in what (God) commands them to do." (66:6)

Angels are the noblest and purest beings. With the command of God, they can make themselves visible in various forms, even to be like a human being, until they have completed their spiritual duties as commanded to do so by God.

The most well-known angel is Jibrail (Gabriel) who is the Archangel. Nicknamed the "Spirit of Faith and Truth" (26:193) and the "Holy Spirit" (16:102), he was given the task of delivering God's Revelations to all the prophets, including Jesus Christ and Prophet Muhammad (2:97), as well as strengthening their faith (2:87) and that of all believers (58:22).

Angels also came to Mary, the mother of Jesus Christ, bringing the news that she had been chosen by God to conceive Jesus Christ (without a male intervention) (3:42–46), and to the mother of Prophet Moses to inform her about the safety of the infant Moses (28:7).

Angels pray for the well-being of all human beings. God says: "The Angels celebrate the praises of their Lord, and pray for forgiveness for all beings on earth." (42:5)

In the Hereafter, angels will greet the people in Heaven with the "*Salam*" (Greeting of Peace). God says: "The Angels will enter (Heaven) from every door, (and say to the people) 'Peace be upon you'. See, how excellent is the final Home!" (13:23–24)

Satan

In the Qur'an, Satan (Shaitan) is referred to as the "Evil One". Satan lives to "excite enmity and hatred" (5:94) among human beings in multifarious ways. Therefore, God advises people: "Follow not the footsteps of the Evil One for he is to you an avowed enemy." (2:208) This is so because Satan had himself vowed that he would "lie in wait for them" (7:16) and "assault them from before them and behind them, from their right and their left" (7:17).

The "assault" of Satan from every direction means that he can approach his victim in any subtle way. God warns: "O you who believe! Follow not Satan's footsteps. If any will follow the footsteps of Satan, he (Satan) will but command what is shameful and wrong." (24:21)

To people who ignored the teachings of God and fell into disgrace, God would ask them: "Did I not warn you, O children of Adam, that you should not worship Satan for he was to you an enemy avowed? … He did lead astray a great multitude of you. Did you not then understand?" (34:60–62)

God assures the believer that Satan will not harm him if he obeys God in ways He has shown in His Guidance. God says: "Whosoever follows My Guidance, on them shall be no fear, nor shall they grieve." (2:38)

Indeed, Satan acknowledges that he will not be able to tempt or harm all sincere and true believers, meaning people who closely follow God's Guidance. God quotes Satan as saying: "By Your Power, I will put all people in the wrong, except those who are sincere and purified (by Your Grace)." (38:83)

ADAM AND EVE

In Islam, the creation of human beings was in God's Plan. His Plan was to have human beings on earth when the earth was ready for human habitation.

The first human beings, Adam and Eve, were created from clay at the same time. Just as human beings are developed for a specified period in the mother's womb before they are delivered into the world, Adam and Eve were placed in a very special and highly suited place for nurturing to take place — Paradise — and then put on earth to procreate and populate the globe.

God gave Adam and Eve a soul, conscience, knowledge and the ability to make choices, all special attributes that were not given to any of His other non-human living creatures. They dwelt in Paradise as husband and wife. When Adam had learnt to follow God's command seriously, his status as the father of mankind was enhanced. The Qur'an says: "His Lord chose him (from His grace); He turned to him and gave him guidance." (20:122) He, thus, became Islam's first prophet.

When Adam and Eve were ready for their worldly roles, God assures Prophet Adam of his prophetic mission: "As is sure, there comes to you Guidance from Me, so whosoever (of your descendants) follows My Guidance, will not lose his way, nor fall into misery." (20:123)

A Hadith (saying or deed of Prophet Muhammad) says that Adam and Eve appeared on earth not far from each other, and so after a short period of wandering, they were re-united at Jabal Rahmah (Mount of Mercy) in the plain of Arafah, a few kilometres away from Mecca.

The plain of Arafah is where all pilgrims congregate during their Haj to listen to the Haj sermon. Mount Rahmah is also where Prophet Muhammad had stood and delivered his sermon during his last pilgrimage, known as the Farewell Pilgrimage.

NATURE OF HUMAN BEINGS

Human beings have been created "in the best form" (95:4) with intelligence, abilities and compassion. God says: "We have endowed them with the faculties of hearing, seeing, heart (feeling) and intellect (understanding)." (23:78) & (46:26)

Islam says that man came into this world with *fitrah* (naturally good and pure state) regardless of whether he was born into a Muslim or non-Muslim family. A baby at birth is pure, innocent and sinless. Prophet Muhammad said that "each child is born with *fitrah*".

Prophet Muhammad explained that, as the child grows up, temptations and negative influences and other external forces influence and change his natural disposition. Islam, therefore, teaches man to maintain his natural disposition as best as he can by doing good and refraining from doing unrighteous acts. God says: "Those who do right and refrain from wrong have a great reward." (3:172)

Unlike the angels (who do good only) and Satan (who does bad only), man, with his intelligence and freedom of choice, can do good and evil, or change from good to evil or vice versa. As such, he can rise to the level of dignity — the angelic level — or fall to the level of degradation — the satanic level. He can act virtuously and reach the zenith of worldly sublimation and spiritual perfection, or act immorally and sink to the deepest pit of disgrace and humiliation. His worldly and spiritual destiny lies in his own hands.

But God, in His mercy and compassion, sent prophets throughout the ages to teach man God's "religion of right" (6:161), one that teaches man to "Serve God and eschew evil" (16:36), so as to give him the opportunity to understand both good and evil and allow him to make his choice.

2 ▲ GOD-GUIDED PATH

"Read! In the name of your Lord." (96:1) This was the very first Revelation, indeed a command, Prophet Muhammad received from God in preparation for his 23-year-long prophetic mission. The Revelations make up the Qur'an, which means "the Reading".

Islam is neither a new religion nor introduced by Prophet Muhammad, but one that has been delivered in developmental stages through the ages by numerous prophets of God. Prophet Muhammad was the final Prophet sent to deliver God's Religion for mankind called "Islam", a word suggesting peace and bliss.

ESTABLISHMENT OF ISLAM

The Hadith (words and deeds of Prophet Muhammad) mentions that God sent more than 124,000 chosen men, commonly called prophets, to various communities in different parts of the earth and at various periods in time. They came to teach and deliver the "religion of right" (6:161), in various stages that suited the people of that time. All the prophets taught the essence of Islam, that is "Serve God and eschew evil." (16:36) God says: "The same religion has He (God) established for you as that which He has enjoined on Noah — that which We (God) have sent by Inspiration to you (O Muhammad), and which We enjoined on Abraham, Moses and Jesus." (42:13)

When the time was finally ripe for the God-sent religion to be completed for universal application — for all people and for all time — God chose Prophet Muhammad for the task. He became "the Seal of the Prophets" (33:40), the final prophet in the long line of chosen men sent by God to guide people.

With the enhancement and completion of the "religion of right", God gave it a name — Islam. God says: "This day I have enhanced your *Deen* (the believers' way of life) for you, completed My favour upon you, and have chosen for you Islam as your religion." (5:4) The "religion of right" was thus formally established with a name.

Islam means "Peace, upheld through total submission to God". It places emphasis on the attainment of the well-being of the believer, both in this world and for the Hereafter. It is a religion for anyone, without any restriction on race or locality. It is for all mankind.

THE STRAIGHT WAY

Islam teaches Muslims to keep a balance between extremes, rejecting both licentiousness and exaggerated self-denial. God says: "This (Islam) is My Way, leading straight; follow it: follow not other paths." (2:256) Anyone deviating from the straight path or straying from it would be exposed to negative temptations.

Islam is the God-guided Straight Way (6:161) to the Hereafter; it is a sort of "fast lane". The very first chapter of the Qur'an, "Al-Fatiha", is a popular *do'a* (supplication) in itself. A short chapter of seven verses only, its fifth and sixth verses go thus: "(Praise be to God ...) You do we worship and Your help do we seek. Guide us on the Straight Way, the way on whom You have bestowed Your Grace..." (1:5–6)

Two meanings are conspicuous in the term "the Straight Way":

- First, the "Straight Way, a religion of right" (6:161) is one that is righteous and desired, embodying universal values such as tolerance, humility and dignity.
- Second, it is a path that is essential for "balanced" living. This path leads Muslims neither to neglect the world and concentrate only on the good of the Hereafter nor to forget the Hereafter and focus only on the good of this world. Islam does not encourage extreme leanings.

Thus, Islam teaches that Muslims ought to be exemplary in their moral conduct and, at the same time, enjoy the earthly life. God says:

- "Do not neglect your share in this world." (28:77)
- "When the *solat* (Islamic prayers) has been performed, disperse

- Saleh (Methuselah)
- Ibrahim (Abraham)
- Luth (Lot)
- Ismail (Ishmael)
- Ishak (Isaac)
- Yakub (Jacob)
- Yusuf (Joseph)
- Shu'aib (Jethro)
- Ayub (Job)
- Zulkifli (Ezekiel)
- Musa (Moses)
- Harun (Aaron)
- Dawud (David)
- Sulaiman (Solomon)
- Ilyas (Elias)
- Al-yasa (Elisha)
- Yunus (Jonah)
- Zakariya (Zachariah)
- Yahya (John, the Baptist)
- Isa (Jesus, the Christ)
- Muhammad

These prophets' names are popular names for Muslims, although some names might be spelt a bit differently, for example Dawud as Dawood, Harun as Haroon, Sulaiman as Sulayman and Muhammad as Mohamad.

4. Belief in the Divine Revelations

Muslims believe in all the Revelations of God to His prophets, such as the *Taurat* (the Torah, the original words of guidance that were revealed to Prophet Moses), the *Zabur* (the Psalms, the original words of guidance that were revealed to Prophet David) and the *Injil* (the Gospel, the original words of guidance that were revealed to Prophet Jesus). (It is to be noted that Muslims do not consider the entire Bible as the *Injil* as it was written by many authors although parts of the *Injil* could have survived in the New Testament). The Qur'an is the original words of guidance revealed to Prophet Muhammad, which he first recited for recording and used to recite often during prayers and other occasions.

5. Belief in the Divine Will of God

Muslims believe in God's knowledge and power. He is Compassionate and Merciful and so whatever He does has a good motive and meaningful purpose for all His creations. Hence, whatever happens, whether it is an untimely death from a car accident or a debilitating disease or chronic health problems, is in the knowledge of God. If there are no accidents, there is no necessity for safety guides and regulations and lawyers to fight cases; if there are no diseases, there is no necessity for doctors and health programmes. But all happy and sad happenings are in the knowledge of God; it is His Will.

6. Belief in life after death and the Day of Judgement

Muslims believe in life after death. Life on earth is meant to be a preparation for the Hereafter, and on the Day of Judgement each person will be judged on how he spent his life on earth. Rewards and punishments will be meted out accordingly with complete justice as God is Just and Merciful.

FIVE PILLARS OF ISLAM

The fundamentals of Islam are five-fold. They are:

1. Shahadah — the Declaration or Testimony of Faith
2. Solat — the five daily obligatory prayers
3. Saum — fasting in the whole month of Ramadan
4. Zakat — the annual tax or obligatory charity for the needy
5. Haj — the annual pilgrimage in Mecca

1. Shahadah

The *Shahadah* comprises the following utterance: "I bear witness that there is no god but God, and I bear witness that Muhammad is His Messenger." The *Shahadah* highlights the belief that the purpose of a Muslim's life is to serve and obey God, and this is achieved through the teachings given in the Qur'an and the Hadith.

2. Solat

Solat is the obligatory prayers that are performed five times a day: at dawn, in the early afternoon, in the late afternoon, just after sunset and at early night. These prayers can be performed in the mosque or at home or in any conducive place, in the direction of Mecca called *qibla*. The Friday noon *solat* is performed in the mosque in congregation. The *solat*, during which chapters from the Qur'an are recited in Arabic, comprises four postures: standing, bowing, prostrating and sitting, done in a number of fixed units called *raka'at*. For example, the *Suboh solat* (the just-after dawn prayer) has two *raka'ats*; *Maghrib* (the just-after dusk prayer) has three *raka'ats*, and each of the other three *solats* has four *raka'ats*.

3. Saum
Saum (abstaining from food and drink and other forms of self-restraint) is observed in the entire month of Ramadan, the ninth month of the Muslim calendar, from dawn to dusk. Not only does the Islamic fasting have health benefits, it is also a method of self-purification and self-restraint. A fasting person focuses on his or her purpose in life by constantly making himself or herself aware of the presence of God. In the Qur'an, God says: "O you who believe! Fasting is prescribed for you as it was prescribed to those before you that you may learn self-restraint." (2:183)

4. Zakat
In Islam, everything belongs to God, and that wealth is held by human beings in trust. Hence, Muslims pay the *zakat*, a form of an annual religious tax or obligatory charity meant for those in need in the society. An individual may also give as much as he or she pleases as *sadaqah* which is voluntary charity.

5. Haj
The pilgrimage in Mecca, called the Haj, is an obligation for those who are physically and financially able to perform it. The Haj is held in Zulhijjah, the twelfth month of the Muslim year. All pilgrims wear similar white robes (black is also permissible for women) that do not distinguish them from the rich or poor or from any status or position, so that everyone stands equal before God. After performing the various rites of the Haj, the pilgrims celebrate Eid ul-Adha (Festival of Sacrifice) before returning to their homeland. Those who are not on the Haj celebrate Eid ul-Adha in their respective countries. The main activity during Eid ul-Adha is the *qurban* or slaughtering of animals like sheep and cattle, the meat of which is distributed to the poor.

3 🕌 THE CREATOR

God, the Creator of the universe, is One. Muslims of any race from any part of the world, be they Arab, English, Chinese, Indian, Malay, French or American, refer to God by one common name as given in the Qur'an — Allah. Allah is the God of all human beings, of all mankind. Muslims learn much about the oneness of God and His attributes from the Qur'an. "God is the Creator of all things: He is the One, the Supreme, the Irresistible." (13:16)

In the Qur'an, God describes Himself marvellously. First, there is a whole but concise, easy-to-read four-verse chapter, Chapter 112 called "Al-Ikhlas" (The Purity of Faith) where He describes Himself, thus:

- Say, "He is God, the One.
- God, the Eternal, Absolute.
- He begets not, nor was He begotten.
- And there is nothing comparable to Him."(112:1-4)

This short and poetic chapter provides a definition of God — that He is One and Only; He has no beginning or end; He does not have a son or a daughter, and that nothing is like Him (that is, God cannot be imagined or made into an image or idol by humans). This chapter, in its original Arabic, is on every Muslim's lips; even Muslim children of five or four years of age can recite it effortlessly.

The name of God is Allah and this name is repeated 2,698 times in different verses throughout the Qur'an. Every chapter of the 114 chapters of the Qur'an, except Chapter 9, starts with the *basmallah*, a short invocation that goes thus: "*Bismillahir Rahmanir Rahim*" ("In the name of Allah, Most Gracious, Most Merciful."). (See Appendix B for how Muslims incorporate the name "Allah" into their daily lives.)

Apart from Chapter 112, people can know God from His Qualities or Attributes described in numerous places throughout the Qur'an. The total number of God's Attributes, called *Asma ul-Husna* (Most Beautiful Names), is 99. An example of a verse that shows God's Attributes is: "He is Allah, besides Whom there is no god except He. He is the King, the Holy, the Giver of Peace, the Guardian, the Almighty, the Irresistible, the Supreme: Glory be to Allah!" (59:23)

The Qur'an says: "The most beautiful names belong to Allah: so call on Him by them." (7:180) Muslims not only often vocalise many of the names of Allah but the 99 names have also been written in calligraphic art form in Arabic script for display in mosques and homes. There is also a beautiful religious song called *"Asma ul-Husna"*, the lyrics of which is the 99 beautiful names of God in Arabic.

The description of God in the Qur'an shows that Prophet Muhammad, an unlettered person, could not have described God so extensively in such sublime ways except God Himself.

GOD'S ATTRIBUTES

God ("Allah" in Islam) is beyond the limited comprehension of human beings. They cannot imagine Him. "No vision can comprehend Him, but He comprehends all vision." (6:103) They can only feel His existence in their hearts.

"Allah" means "the God". When Muslims of any race, hailing from any corner of the globe, mention "Allah", they understand that He (God):

- is not a female or male.
- needs no wife, son or daughter.
- needs no partner to assist Him.
- does not exist in any physical form, giant-like or human-like, or as a man-made image.
- does not need to become or be born as a human being to experience human life.
- has no beginning and therefore was not born somewhere on earth or elsewhere in the universe.
- has no end and therefore will not die but exist forever.

Muslims understand God's nature and characteristics by His attributes mentioned in the Qur'an, such as the Creator, the Supreme, the Merciful, the Eternal and the Nourisher. This is known as *Asma ul-Husna*. God has many names that indicate His transcendent majesty and uniqueness. In the Qur'an, 99 of these most beautiful and popular names are mentioned, with "Allah" capping them all as the hundredth.

God's attributes are mentioned throughout the Qur'an and are frequently repeated in different context for emphasis and reminder. For example, in mentioning that God is the Creator of the universe, God says: "He is the Creator of the heavens and the earth. To Him belongs the keys of the heavens and the earth." (42:11–12) "Heavens" in this verse, written in the lower case, refers to the entire universe and everything orbiting in it, including the galaxies, planets and stars.

Another verse goes thus: "God! There is no god but He — the Living, the Self-subsisting, Eternal, no slumber can seize Him, nor sleep. His are all things in the heavens and on earth ... He knows all that lies open before men and all that is hidden from them ... His throne extends over the heavens and the earth, and he feels no fatigue in creating and preserving them. For He is the Most High, the Supreme (in glory)." (2:255) From this verse alone, a believer learns:

- five more attributes of God, namely, the Living, the Self-subsisting, the Eternal, the Most High and the Supreme.
- that God does not sleep or feel sleepy.
- that everything in the universe belongs to God.
- that God does not get fatigued (tired) in His work and therefore needs no rest at all.
- that God knows everything.
- that God continues with His creating process.
- that God preserves His creation.

In another verse, it is indicated that "God created (out of nothing) the heavens and the earth. He adds to Creation as He pleases: for God has power over all things." (35:1) In this verse, the complexities of the creative processes are referred to. It shows that God's creation did not stop at some past time but continues (as proven by science today that the universe is not static but changing).

God also provides a precise and concise description of Himself: "He is God, the One and Only; God, the Eternal, the Absolute; He begets not, nor is He begotten; and there is none like Him." (112:1– 4) In these four short verses, some other information about God is given:

- that God is One and Only (that is, He is the God of every human being).
- that God is also called the Absolute ("Absolute" is another of God's attributes).
- that God does not require a son or children.
- that God is not the son of anybody (otherwise there will be another god greater than God!). In another verse, God says that if there were two gods, there will be chaos in the universe.
- that God does not look like anyone or anything. As such Muslims do not paint pictures depicting God or make statues or images of Him.

God is "exalted in power, full of wisdom" (45:37) and is "the Cherisher and Sustainer of the universe, Most Gracious, Most Merciful …" (1:1–3)

GOD'S COMPASSION
Numerous verses in the Qur'an mention that God is compassionate, merciful, gracious and forgiving, indicating that He loves all living and non-living things that He has created, is creating or will create.

God greatly loves human beings, and this is particularly reflected in verses such as:

- "I am indeed close to them: I listen to the prayer of every supplicant when he calls on Me." (2:186)
- "Verily, the help of God is always near." (2:214)
- "Verily God is full of Grace and Bounty to mankind." (40:61)

God's love for human beings is so overpowering that He assures them in an endearing manner thus: "If anyone does evil or wrongs his own soul but afterwards seeks God's forgiveness, he will find God Oft-forgiving, Most Merciful." (4:110)

GOD'S KNOWLEDGE

God knows everything, even a person's intentions. God is "the All-Hearing, All-Knowing" (2:137) and He is "full of knowledge and is acquainted with all things" (31:34).

Qur'anic statements that indicate that God knows everything often appear at the end of verses to support the information given in the verses, for example:

- "In the end, to your Lord is your return, when He will tell you the truth of all you did in this life. For He knows well all that is in (men's) hearts." (39:7)
- "If any one desires a reward in this life, in God's (gift) is the reward both of this life and of the Hereafter. For God is He that hears and sees all things." (4:113)

God knows whatever a person does, his secret thoughts and motives and even his inner feelings. The Qur'an indicates:

- "From God, verily nothing is hidden on earth or in the heavens." (3:5)
- "They may hide their crimes from men but they cannot hide them from God." (4:108)
- "God knows well the secrets in your hearts." (5:8)

As the Creator of everything in the cosmos, "God sees and hears all things" (5:79) and "knows the unseen" (13:9). God therefore offers His Guidance to human beings for their own good.

GOD'S GUIDANCE

There are many statements in the Qur'an that emphasise the importance and benefits of God's Guidance. Three of them are:

- "Whosoever follows My Guidance, on them shall be no fear, nor shall they grieve." (2:38)
- "Whoever follows My Guidance will not lose his way (the righteous way as shown by God), nor fall into misery." (20:123)
- "If any accepts (My) Guidance, they do it for the good of their own souls." (27:92)

God's Guidance enables the believer to start out in the right direction in all his social dealings, economic endeavours and intellectual pursuits. The Guidance provided in the Qur'an is in the form of precepts. One set of such Guidance appears in verse 177 of Chapter 2 of the Qur'an, as follows:

- "It is righteous to believe in God, and the Last Day, and the Angels, and the Book (the Qur'an), and the Prophets (including Prophet Abraham, Prophet Moses, Prophet Noah, Jesus Christ and Prophet Muhammad);
- Spend your substance (monetary or non-monetary) out of love for God, for your kin, for orphans, for the needy, for the wayfarer, for those who ask (not only for beggars but also for emergencies, disasters and fund-collection for any good cause);
- Be steadfast in *solat*;
- Practise regular charity (regular donations to those in need);
- Fulfil the contracts you made (verbal or written promises);
- Be firm and patient in pain or suffering and adversity and throughout all periods of panic (perseverance in any hardship) ..." (2:177)

The injunctions contained in the above verse can be categorised under three broad areas of man's activities as follows:

- religious beliefs and practices
- social relations
- self-discipline

The first category regulates man's relationship to his Creator. This includes the Six Articles of Faith and the Five Pillars of Islam which serve as the basis of all Islamic theological activities, such as belief in the Qur'an and performing the *solat*.

The second set of injunctions emphasises the need to share one's fortune with the less fortunate members of society, keep one's promises to others, promote the well-being of the society, and establish cordial and peaceful co-existence among all human beings, irrespective of race, culture or religion.

The third precept mentions that man must be patient and face up to the problems of life with determination.

Some other guidance on righteous living in Chapter 2 of the Qur'an includes:

- "Make no mischief on earth." (2:11)
- "Practise right conduct." (2:44)
- "(i) Worship none but God, (ii) Treat with kindness your parents and kindred, and orphans and those in need, and (iii) Speak fair to people …" (2:83)
- "Seek help with patient perseverance." (2:153)
- "Eat what is *halal* (lawful) and good." (2:168)
- "Fast in Ramadan." (2:183–185)
- "Do not eat up properties of others." (2:188)
- "Do not transgress limits (of justice or fair dealings)." (2:190)
- "Do good." (2:195)
- "Perform Haj and Umrah (minor pilgrimage)." (2:196)
- "Do not drink alcohol or gamble." (2:219)
- "Keep yourself pure and clean (by keeping away from negative temptations and sins)." (2:222)
- "Provide maintenance to your former wife (in a divorce case)." (2:241)
- "There is no compulsion in religion." (2:256)
- "Give of the good things of which you have honourably earned." (That is, do not give to charity what is to be discarded or acquired in a shameful way.) (2:267)
- "Do not indulge in usury." (2:278)
- "Grant time to the debtor who is in difficulty till it is easy for him to repay." (That is, do not squeeze his neck if he is unable to pay promptly.) (2:280)
- "Conceal not evidence (in cases where evidence of truth is required)." (2:283)

The examples of guidance given in just one verse of 2:177 and in many other verses in Chapter 2 are not the only places where Islamic instructions are given. Here are some examples of guidance given throughout the Qur'an:

- Restrain anger (3:134)
- Do not be rude in speech (3:159)
- Women also have the right for inheritance (4:7)

- Wealth of the dead should be distributed among his family members (4:7)
- Do not devour the property of orphans (4:10)
- Do not consume one another's wealth unjustly (4:29)
- Be good to others (4:36)
- Judge with justice between people (4:58)
- Stand out firmly for justice (4:135)
- Do not insult others' deities (6:108)
- Do not be arrogant (7:13)
- Forgive others for their mistakes (7:199)
- Be dutiful to parents (17:23)
- Do not say a word of disrespect to parents (17:23)
- Speak to people mildly (20:44)
- Do not enter parents' private room without asking permission (24:58)
- Walk on earth in humility (25:63)
- Do not be a boaster (31:18)
- Do not ridicule others (49:11)
- Save yourself from covetousness (64:16)

God provides guidance in every aspect of the believer's life, showing how he should live and extend his relations with God, fellow human beings and the environment.

As "the Protector of those who have faith" (2:257), God instructs them to always seek His help and forgiveness. A popular Qur'anic *do'a* (supplication) that Muslims often say is: "Our Lord! Lay not on us a burden greater than we have strength to bear. Blot out our sins, and grant us forgiveness. Have mercy on us. You are our Protector." (2:286)

4 🕌 BEARERS OF GOOD NEWS

From the time of the first pair of human beings, Adam and Eve, God has sent a long line of chosen men, commonly called prophets, as bearers of the good news of God. They came to instruct people to believe in God and to be righteous. The last of these prophets was Prophet Muhammad. He was the final or "Seal of the prophets" (33:40), sent to complete the "Straight Way, a religion of right" (6:161) and establish Islam.

PROPHETS THROUGH THE AGES

Muslims believe in all the earlier prophets of God such as Prophet Adam, Prophet Abraham, Prophet Noah, Prophet Moses and Prophet Jesus (who is referred to as "Jesus Christ, son of Mary" in the Qur'an).

Islam says that ever since the existence of human life on earth, God has sent more than 124,000 chosen men (as mentioned in the Hadith) to various parts of the world, at various periods of time, to various communities of people to guide them towards righteous living. These chosen men are termed variously as apostles, messengers, prophets and warners in the Qur'an. God says:

- "To every nation was sent an Apostle." (10:47)
- "There was never a people without a Warner having lived among them (in the past)." (35:24)

Regarding their mission, God says: "We sent prophets save as bearers of good news and to warn: so those who believe and mend their lives — upon them shall be no fear, nor shall they grieve." (6:48) The Qur'an mentions 25 of the prophets by name (see pages 24–25 for the names of the prophets). They are mentioned when God relates certain matters regarding their roles.

Prophets were people with exceptional upright character. In his book *Islam, the Basic Truths*, Gaafar S. Idris says about prophets: "They are men of extremely high moral, spiritual and intellectual standards that qualify them — in the eyes of God — to be the bearers of His 'Lights' to the world. When God chooses any of them, He supports him with a clear 'sign' that proves the truth of his claim, and distinguishes him from false prophets, sorcerers and soothsayers. None of them betrays the Message or falls short of being exemplary in practising what he preaches."

JESUS CHRIST

Prophet Jesus is referred as the "Masih" (Christ) in the Qur'an, a special title meaning the "anointed one". He was every bit a human being just as all the other prophets, including Prophet Abraham, Prophet Moses and Prophet Muhammad. About his nature and mission, God says:

- "Christ, the son of Mary, was no more than a prophet; many were the prophets that passed away before him." (5:78)
- "We sent Jesus, the son of Mary, the Gospel: therein was guidance and light and confirmation of the Law that had come before him." (5:49)

The Qur'an mentions a great deal about Jesus Christ. The information about him includes:

- He was conceived miraculously: Jesus Christ was conceived by Mary without a male intervention (3:45–47).
- He was sent for the people of Israel: God appoints him as "a prophet to the children of Israel" (3:49).
- God equipped him with Divine Knowledge: God says that He taught him "the Book and Wisdom, the Law and the Gospel" (3:48).
- He performed miracles as permitted by God: Jesus Christ performed all his miracles "by My leave" (5:113), meaning by God's permission or authority just as Prophet Moses performed his miracles, also by God's "leave".

- He worshipped God: Like all the other prophets, he worshipped God and taught people to worship God. The Qur'an quotes Jesus Christ as saying: "O Children of Israel! Worship God, my Lord and your Lord" (5:75) because "there is no god except One God" (5:76).

Mary, a firm believer of the One God, is described in the Qur'an as a pious and virtuous woman, coming from a very religious family.

God sent angels to inform Mary that she had been specially chosen to conceive Jesus Christ who would later become a great prophet. "Behold!" the angels said: "O Mary! God has chosen you above the women of all nations." (3:42)

The angels told her that her son would be called Jesus and held highly by people and God: "O Mary! God gives you glad tidings of a word from Him: his name will be Jesus, the son of Mary, held in honour in this world and the Hereafter and (of the company of) those nearest to God." (3:46)

Upon receiving this news, although a piece of good news, Mary was shocked as no woman had ever conceived a baby without a male intervention. Mary, responding in a most polite way befitting her moral standing, asked God: "O My Lord! How shall I have a son when no man has touched me?" He replied: "Even so: God creates what he wills: When He has decreed a Plan, He but says to it, 'Be' and it is." (3:47–48)

The conception of Jesus Christ was made possible by the power of God. God need only say "Be" and it happens, just as Adam was created without even a mother! God says: "The similitude of Jesus before God is as that of Adam; He created him from dust, then said to him: 'Be' and he was." (3:59)

Muslims revere, respect and love Jesus Christ as they do to Prophet Muhammad and all the other prophets before him.

PROPHET MUHAMMAD

Prophet Muhammad was born on 29 August 570 in Mecca. His father, Abdullah, died before he was born. His mother, Aminah, died when he was six years old. His grandfather, Abdul Mutalib, who became his guardian, died when he was eight. He was then taken care of by one of his uncles, Abu Talib, in whose house he grew up.

Even in his youth, the Prophet's pure character and his regard for truth and honesty won him the title "Al-Amin" (the trustworthy) and "As-Saadiq" (the truthful) from people of his hometown.

In his early twenties, Muhammad came into the service of Khadijah, a rich and upright widow, who employed him as one of her staff in her trading business. She was so greatly impressed with his conduct and sense of responsibility that she offered him her hand in marriage, although she was 15 years his senior. Muhammad accepted the proposal and they were married. He was 25 years old at the time.

Muhammad received prophethood at the age of 40. "Read! In the name of your Lord…" (96:1) was the very first instruction he received from God. From that auspicious day, he received God's message (the Qur'an) in small, manageable portions from time to time over 23 years.

As a Messenger of God, Prophet Muhammad's mission was to deliver the Message of God to people. He was not responsible if people would not believe in the Message (Islam) he delivered. It is up to the people to scrutinise the Message he delivered and accept it if it is rational. God says: "Let there be no compulsion in religion: Truth stands out clear from error." (2:256)

Prophet Muhammad, as the final Prophet for mankind, came to:

- reiterate and enforce the unity of God as taught by the earlier prophets — that there is only One God and worship is due to Him only.
- establish the brotherhood of mankind.
- establish Islam as the "completed and perfected" (5:4) religion for all mankind.
- deliver the Qur'an to mankind, and ensure the authenticity of it in the written form.

Islam is a universal religion and Prophet Muhammad was sent for all people, irrespective of race and colour. God informs the Prophet of his mission, thus:

- "We have sent you as an Apostle to instruct mankind." (4:79)
- "We sent you not, but as a Mercy for mankind." (21:107)
- "O Prophet! Truly We sent you as a Witness, a Bearer of Glad Tidings and a Warner and as one who invites (people) to God's Grace." (33:45–46)

Immediately upon completing his mission, the Prophet performed his last pilgrimage that became known as the Farewell Pilgrimage. In his sermon of that pilgrimage, he assured Muslims that they would be successful if they hold fast to the Qur'an and the *Sunnah* (conduct of the Prophet). He said: "I leave behind two things, the Qur'an and my example (the *Sunnah*), and if you follow these you will never go astray."

Shortly after performing this pilgrimage, the Prophet passed away, at the age of 63.

PERSECUTION

The story of Prophet Muhammad would be incomplete without mentioning the most trying and challenging period of his life — his persecution which resulted in his migration to Medina. The migration of the Prophet from Mecca to Medina is a milestone event in Islamic history. It is a story of patience, endurance, striving and eventual triumph in the face of seemingly extreme hopelessness.

The Prophet lived at a time when the Arab society was in a state of marked corruption and decay and in the grips of the worst form of idolatry. So, when the Prophet began delivering the Message of Islam to the Arabs, they opposed him.

The pagan Arabs worshipped numerous deities; they were fierce alcoholics; they practised infanticide (they killed female babies); and they treated women as mere chattels. On the other hand, Islam advocated the worship of One God, prohibited alcohol, banned infanticide, condemned superstition and gave rights to women. All these and other positive changes made the pagans feel that their culture and traditions were being destroyed by Islam. However, there were some people who saw Islam's beauty and became Muslims. This made the pagans turn on them, forcing them to abandon the religion. But the converts remained firm.

The pagans then approached the Prophet's uncle and guardian, Abu Talib, and urged him to force his nephew to stop his preaching. They were willing to offer the Prophet wealth and status in return. When Abu Talib told this to him, the Prophet said: "O Uncle, if they could place the moon on my left hand and the sun on my right, I would still not give up the mission entrusted upon me by God."

The persecution of the Muslims thus intensified — many were tortured; many were killed.

For 13 years, the Prophet carried on with his mission patiently, bearing all the agony and hardship of the persecution. At one point, for the safety of his followers, he sent some of them to Abyssinia, a country whose devout Christian king gave them refuge on the basis that the fundamentals of his religion and those of Islam were almost the same.

One day, some visiting traders from Yathrib, an oasis town about 500 kilometres north of Mecca, embraced Islam after having listened to Prophet Muhammad's preaching. The following year, these same Yathribites returned, bringing another group of their fellow citizens. All pledged their loyalty to the Prophet. When they left, they even took with them a companion of the Prophet to teach their fellow citizens back home the fundamentals of Islam. As a result, Islam spread in Yathrib.

The pagan Arabs became even more furious when they learnt about the spread of Islam in Yathrib. They now threatened to kill the Prophet and his followers in Mecca. On the appointed night when the assassins burst into the Prophet's room, they realised that he had given them the slip. His destination was Yathrib.

Horsemen were despatched immediately to hunt him down. Rewards of a hundred camels were announced for his capture — dead or alive — and bounty hunters eagerly searched the deserts around Mecca. For several days the Prophet and his companion, Abu Bakar, hid in a cave in Jabal Thaur, a mountain some six kilometres from Mecca. Once or twice they even heard voices of their enemies outside the cave. Knowing that a mere glance into the cave would have been sufficient to end their lives, Abu Bakar whispered: "What can we do, we are only two." But the Prophet consoled his companion with the words: "Do not grieve, God is surely with us." (9:40)

Then, with the help of a camel guide, the Prophet and Abu Bakar started on the long and arduous 500-kilometre journey across the burning, hostile desert to Yathrib. This historic journey to a friendly place is called the "Hijrah".

On 2 July of the year 622, the Prophet stepped onto the soil of Yathrib. This oasis town henceforth became known as Medinatul Nabi (City of the Prophet) or simply Medina.

Here, the Prophet gave form and continuity to the Muslim community and the state with all the various elements of social, economic and political life he had been commanded by God to establish. From Medina, the first Islamic state, the religion rapidly spread throughout Arabia.

After 10 years in Medina, the Prophet decided to visit his beloved Mecca, the place of his birth, now still in the hands of his enemies. With 10,000 Muslims, he entered Mecca — without any resistance or bloodshed. The Prophet freely forgave all his enemies.

The Hijrah is significant in the life of a Muslim because it highlights the accomplishment of a goal by way of a change in strategy. It signifies growth, progress and success.

5 🕌DIVINE MESSAGES

God has sent more than 124,000 prophets since human beings appeared on earth to guide people to the path of God. In the early stages of civilisation, they came to deliver moral teachings, and in the later stages, the succeeding prophets taught not only morals but philosophical precepts and religious laws.

Among those who delivered religious laws were Prophet David (the Psalms or *Zabur*), Prophet Moses (the Law or the Torah (*Taurat*)), Jesus Christ (the Gospel or *Injil*) and Prophet Muhammad (the Qur'an).

MESSAGES OF PROPHETS

Prophets received Messages termed "Revelations" from God that formed the basis of their teachings. God gave the same fundamental Messages to all his prophets for delivery to their respective people. Basically, all their Messages advocated the same core teaching — that God is One and that people should worship God alone and be righteous.

The Qur'an (delivered by Prophet Muhammad) confirms the validity of the earlier Revelations. The following two verses bear this out:

- "It is He (God) who sent down the Book (the Qur'an) confirming what went before it; and He sent down the Law (of Moses) and the Gospel (of Jesus) before this, as a guide to mankind." (3:3)
- "This is a Book (the Qur'an) which We have sent down, bringing Blessings and confirming (the Revelations) which came before it." (6:92)

The Qur'an, being the Final Revealed Book, has always been in the hands and memories of Muslims ever since it was recorded during the time of the Prophet.

Basically, the spoken words of the prophets who delivered the Revelations they received from God make up the Divine Messages, whether these were recorded or not. Those recorded were done to ensure uniformity in teachings, especially after the death of the prophets. Revelations received by the early prophets were verbal and not recorded. Other Revelations were recorded years after the death of the prophets by people claiming to have heard them from the prophets themselves or from someone who had heard of them; usually discrepancies, mistakes and later editings would result in such cases. In the case of the Qur'an, the Revelations were recorded verbatim. Prophet Muhammad requested scribes to record the Revelations, often immediately upon receiving them, and then asked the scribes to read what they had recorded to ascertain accuracy. The whole of the Qur'an had been accomplished in this way in the lifetime of the Prophet.

Muslims therefore follow mainly the teachings given in the Qur'an. God says that the Qur'an is "a Guide, a Mercy and Glad Tidings to Muslims" (16:89) and that "in it is Guidance sure" (2:2). God also says that the Qur'an "is a Clear Message for mankind: Let them take warning therefrom, and let them know that He is (no other than the) One God: Let men of understanding take heed." (14:52)

THE QUR'AN AND THE HADITH

Apart from the Qur'an, there is another book that Muslims rely on for guidance — the Hadith, which contains the words and deeds of the Prophet. The Islamic law and the teachings of Islam are formulated mainly from the Qur'an and the Hadith.

The Qur'an contains the exact Words of God, while the Hadith contains the words and the conduct of Prophet Muhammad. The conduct of the Prophet is called the *Sunnah*. It is from the *Sunnah* that Muslims learn many practical applications of the Qur'an.

The words of these two sources are kept separate to avoid getting them mixed up for the simple reason that the Words of the Qur'an are of divine origin, while the words in the Hadith are God-inspired words of the Prophet reported by people who knew him closely, such as his companions.

While the Qur'an provides guidelines for righteousness, warnings against evil and laws for responsible living, the *Sunnah* shows the Prophet's character and deeds. Together, the Qur'an and the Hadith provide complete guidance for anyone to live a happy life on earth while preparing for the Hereafter.

While the Prophet specifically initiated the Divine Words, as they came to him, to be recorded verbatim as the Qur'an, he did not request his own words and actions on any issue to be recorded for fear that his sayings would be mistaken as Divine Revelations. However, the Prophet did not forbid his companions from recording his sayings to aid their memory as long as they did not regard his personal words as the Words of God. In this way, Muslims have recourse to receiving guidance for their everyday living not only from the Qur'an but also from the *Sunnah*.

The Qur'an carries no acknowledgement of any human name as its author for the simple reason that there is no human author. God is the Author of the whole Qur'an. An illustrative indication to this process may be like the boss of a company who dictates his messages to his secretary, who takes the dictation down verbatim on paper for circulation to the staff. In this example, it is clear that the boss is the author of the messages, not his secretary who merely reproduced them for mass circulation.

The Qur'an is one great Book comprising 114 chapters contained in just one volume. As for the Hadith, each saying or deed of the Prophet carries the name of the person who reported it. The Hadith, classified according to subject matter, is available in a number of volumes.

The fact that the Qur'an comprises the Words of God and the Hadith the words of the Prophet is clear from the distinct style and language used in each of them. The former, being God's Words, is inimitable, while the latter, being the words of Prophet Muhammad reported by people, is ordinary.

The Prophet received the first Divine Revelation when he was 40 years old. In the next 23 years, he modelled a way of life as inspired by the Qur'an. His practical life was not a mere private and secret code of conduct but detailed interpretations and application of the Divine Message known to all. Thus, to obey the Prophet also means to follow his practices and teachings which are recorded in the Hadith. God instructs the Prophet to tell people: "If you do love God, follow me: God will love you." (3:31)

As the Messenger of God, the Prophet showed how certain Qur'anic commands have to be practised. For example, regarding certain religious practices, like the *solat*, the Qur'an mentions it as binding on Muslims. God says: "Enjoin *solat* on your people (O Muhammad!)." (20:132) The Prophet then showed the Muslims how the prayers were to be performed. He said: "Look at me, see how I perform the *solat*, and follow me." And so, Muslims learnt from the Prophet how the *solat* had to be performed. This action or *Sunnah* is recorded in the Hadith.

The *Sunnah* and words of the Prophet as recorded in the Hadith serve as a practical guide and explanation to the correct understanding of the principles set out in the Qur'an. The Prophet, in the sermon of his Farewell Pilgrimage, stressed the importance of these two sources in guiding people. He said: "I leave behind two things, the Qur'an and my example (the *Sunnah*), and if you follow these you will never go astray." (See Appendix C, "The Last Sermon of Prophet Muhammad".)

REVELATIONS OF THE QUR'AN

The Revelations received by Prophet Muhammad is the Qur'an. God assures mankind: "Verily, this is a Revelation from the Lord of the worlds." (26:192) A Revelation may include ideas, knowledge, elucidation, instructions, advice and guidance. Thus, in the Qur'an, God directly addresses four sets of people:

• Prophet Muhammad, as an instruction or an explanation to strengthen his confidence in his mission.
• Muslims in particular.
• believers (in God) in general.
• all mankind.

However, anyone, even a non-believer, reading the Qur'an receives instruction and wisdom from the Revelations directed to any of the four sets of people.

The Archangel Gabriel was the angel entrusted to convey God's Revelations to each and everyone of God's prophets, including Prophet Abraham, Prophet Moses and Jesus Christ. God informs Prophet Muhammad: "(It is) Gabriel (who) brings down the Revelation to your heart by God's will ... (as) guidance and glad tidings for those who believe." (2:97)

The very first Revelation of the Qur'an received by Prophet Muhammad was the instruction to rehearse a five-verse Revelation. It begins: "Read! In the name of your Lord ..." (96:1)

The Prophet received the entire Revelations of the Qur'an over 23 years. Sometimes the Prophet received a single verse, sometimes a few verses together, and sometimes an entire chapter. The Prophet received the Revelations at any time of the day or night, even when he was with his companions.

When receiving a Revelation, Prophet Muhammad would remain quiet, visibly overwhelmed. The Prophet, who was unlettered, would ask anyone of his companions who was literate, or a scribe, to record the Revelation. He would recite the Revelation and the scribe would take it down. After the Revelation had been written, he would ask the scribe to read the text aloud. This was to ensure that the recording was accurate and exactly as he had dictated. The Prophet would then ask his companions to memorise the Revelation, and he would keep the recorded portion for reference. Thus, the text of today's copies of the Qur'an (in Arabic) is the same as that of the first copy — the one seen by the Prophet himself.

The Prophet received the final Revelation a few months before he passed away. It reads: "This day I have perfected your religion for you, completed My favour upon you, and have chosen for you Islam as your religion." (5:4)

In one of the Revelations, God assures believers that He would make sure that the Qur'an will remain unadulterated forever: "We have sent down the Message and We will assuredly guard it from corruption." (15:9)

ROLE OF THE QUR'AN

The Qur'an is a Book of Guidance for everybody. The role of the Qur'an is to help create the right relation between man and God, between man and man, and between man and his environment as well as other things in the universe so that mankind can attain the highest goals in every field of human endeavour — spiritual, moral, scientific, intellectual and social. God tells Prophet Muhammad that the Qur'an is "A Book that We have revealed to you abounding in good. People may ponder over its verses, and that people of understanding may mind." (38:29)

The Qur'an, as a Book of Guidance, provides immense stimulus for man to tap the three important sources of knowledge — self, human history and the physical world — for him to benefit from them. It also provides the principles and rules for gracious living and invites man to carry on discovering the bounties of God for their benefit.

Addressing the Prophet, God says: "Verily, We have revealed the Book (the Qur'an) to you (O Muhammad) in truth for (instructing) mankind. He who receives Guidance (from it) benefits his own soul: but he that strays injures his own soul." (39:41)

The Qur'an, which describes itself as the "Message" and the "Final Message", meaning that no Divine Book will come after it, mentions that it "is nothing less than a Message to all (people)" (68:52). Therefore, as a Final Testament, the Qur'an addresses not only Muslims but also all human beings.

FEATURES OF THE QUR'AN

The Qur'an, a "Revelation from the Lord of the worlds" (56:80), is in Arabic. Translations of the Qur'an are not called "Qur'an". For instance, the translation by Abdullah Yusuf Ali, which contains both the Arabic text and the English translation as well as commentaries, is entitled *The Meaning of the Glorious Qur'an*.

The Qur'an, rendered in prose-poetic style, comprises 6,666 verses spread over 114 chapters. It starts with a seven-verse chapter called "Al-Fatiha" which means "The Opening (Chapter)". The very first verse of this first chapter begins with the *basmallah* (invocation), a three-word verse that goes thus: *"Bismillahir Rahmanir Rahim"* ("In the name of Allah, Most Gracious, Most Merciful.") (1:1) This opening chapter provides the essence or gist of the whole Book and sums up marvellously man's relation to God. The other chapters of the Qur'an, too, except Chapter 9, immediately after the mention of the name of the chapter, begins with this highly devotional invocation. Muslims are encouraged to invoke God's name not only when they begin reading the Qur'an but also when they begin doing other activities like eating, leaving the home for work or making a public speech. The invocation is also written out in official letters as done by Prophet Solomon in his letter to the Queen of Saba' (Sheba) as mentioned in the Qur'an (27:30).

The chapters of the Qur'an were arranged by Prophet Muhammad himself through Divine Guidance, that is, with the help of the Archangel

Gabriel. They were arranged in the order of divine preference, not in chronological order. For instance, the first five verses the Prophet received, which begin with "Read! In the name of your Lord ...", are not in Chapter 1 but in Chapter 96.

Each chapter of the Qur'an has a title. For example, Chapter 9 is called "At-Tauba" ("Repentance") and Chapter 107 is called "Al-Ma'un" ("Neighbourly Needs"). There is also a chapter, Chapter 19, called "Maryam" ("Mary"). This chapter talks about the story of Mary, her ancestors and Jesus Christ.

The word "Qur'an", which means "that which is read" or "The Reading", is frequently mentioned in the Qur'an itself and is applicable to the whole Book as well as to any part of its text. A God-given name, the Qur'an also calls itself "the Book", "the Word", "the Message", "the Revelation", and describes itself at numerous places throughout the Qur'an in the following ways:

- "This is indeed a Book most honourable, a Book well-guarded ... a Revelation from the Lord of the worlds." (56:77–80)
- "Do they not consider (ponder over) the Qur'an? Had it been from other than God, they would surely have found therein discrepancies." (4:82)
- "We have explained in detail in the Qur'an, for the benefit of mankind, every kind of similitude." (18:54)
- "The Book which explains all things, is a Guide, a Mercy and Glad Tidings to Muslims." (16:89)

The Qur'an employs a presentation technique that is unique. First, the Qur'an does not narrate stories like in a history book with themes under the respective chapters. Instead, only the relevant accounts of history, people and prophets are presented and told in such a way that lessons from them can be easily learnt. Second, a person can receive Qur'anic instructions by reading from any page or verse. He need not start from the beginning of the Qur'an or a fresh chapter.

Also, a very special feature of the Qur'an is that any advice or command given is mentioned not once but repeated in different forms and ways at several places in the Qur'an. This methodology ensures grasp and attention. If a reader were to miss reading an advice or command from one place, he would surely come upon it in some other places as he proceeds to read the Book. God does not want the reader to miss out on any information because the Qur'an is not an ordinary book but "It is a Guide and Healing to those who believe" (41:44) and "Verily, in this Qur'an is a Message for people who would truly worship God." (21:106)

ELOQUENT AND LIVING LANGUAGE

The Qur'an is in Arabic, the language spoken by Prophet Muhammad and his community. It was revealed in Arabic for the Prophet's understanding,

As the Qur'an was first sent down to people who spoke Arabic, God sent His Book in a language that would be understood by the Arabs first. God informs Prophet Muhammad: "We have made the Qur'an easy in your own tongue, so that with it you may give glad tidings to the righteous, and warnings to people given to contention." (19:97) The Qur'an states further: "We have sent the Qur'an in Arabic in order that you (or anyone) may learn wisdom." (12:2)

Indeed because of this language facility that affords understanding of the Qur'anic Messages, it was the Prophet's own people, the Arabs, who embraced Islam first before it spread outside the Arabian Peninsula. What is more, the first person in the family to become a Muslim through Islam was the Prophet's own wife, Khadijah. The Prophet's cousin, Ali, and his uncle, Hamza, also became Muslims in the early stages of Islam; so too the Prophet's closest companions, Abu Bakar, Umar and Othman. His other close companions also became Muslims. In fact, in Medina alone, a huge number of men and women converted to Islam. Indeed, when the Prophet re-entered Mecca after 10 years in Medina, he came to Mecca with more than 10,000 of his followers, all dressed in *ihram* (Haj attire) to perform the very first Haj under Islam.

Muslims believe that, just as it was for Prophet Muhammad, all prophets of God, including Prophet Moses and Prophet Jesus, received the Revelations of God through the Angel Gabriel in their own language or dialect so that they would understand the Revelations before transmitting the teachings to their followers.

Arabic, the original language of the Qur'an, is not only an eloquent language to be used for a Divine Book but it is an international, living language today. Millions of people around the world use it — Malays know Arabic, as do millions of Indonesian Muslims, Indian Muslims and Chinese Muslims, apart from the Middle-East Arabs themselves.

Arabic has even influenced other languages like Urdu, Turkish, Iranian and other Central and South-east Asian languages, including Malay. The Malays, aside from the Romanised script, also use the Arabic script in their writings, called Jawi.

The Arabic script also lends itself to artistry and calligraphy. In the past 14 centuries, verses from the Qur'an have been produced in stunning Islamic calligraphic forms to decorate walls and pillars of mosques around the world and as wall-hangings in Muslim homes and shops. As it is considered sacrilegious to depict God (whose form is not physical) or Prophet Muhammad in pictorial forms, Muslims have produced the names "God" and "Muhammad" from Arabic letters in attractive calligraphic artwork, to be hung on the walls of Muslim homes and mosques as decoration.

SOUND OF THE QUR'AN

The sound of the Qur'an is astounding and pleasant to the ears. The verses can be read plainly or recited in a uniquely melodious way with baritone delivery style and intonation.

The beauty of the Qur'an is that the tone and melody can be rendered in many different ways. Non-Muslims who have never heard the sound of the Qur'an can easily watch videos of adults and children reading and reciting the Qur'an on YouTube (type in "Qur'an recital"). Some non-Muslims (on Youtube "Qur'an discovery" clips in London), upon hearing the Qur'anic verses for the first time, say it sounds amazingly pleasant and soothing.

Most Muslims would have already learnt to read the Qur'an before they reach their mid-teens, from Qur'an reading classes held in mosques, *madrasahs* (religious schools) and Muslim organisations. Learning to read the Qur'an is part of their religious upbringing.

As the Qur'an is rendered in prose-poetry style, it can be read in a very enlivened and inspiring way. No musical instrument is needed to accompany the person reading the Qur'an. Referring to the "melody" of the Qur'an, Muhammad Marmaduke Pickthall, in the "Translator's Foreword" of his English translation of the Qur'an, says: "... that inimitable symphony, the very sounds of which move men to tears and ecstasy."

The recitation of the Qur'an in melodious ways has evolved into a sophisticated discipline. Many countries hold annual Qur'an reading competitions to promote recital skills and to pick up the best contestants to participate in national, regional and international Qur'an reading competitions held all over the world for men and women.

VOWEL MARKINGS OF THE QUR'AN
At the time when Prophet Muhammad passed away, although the Revelations of the Qur'an received by him had been recorded, they had not been bound into one volume. The entire Qur'an was in the heart of the Prophet's companions who recited verses and chapters of it from memory when teaching others.

It was the Prophet's successor, Caliph Abu Bakar, himself a close companion, who requested Zayd bin Thabit to bind all the 114 chapters of the Qur'an into one volume, to prevent the chapters from being used individually. Zayd was chosen because it was he who had recorded most of the Prophet's dictation of the Revelations. The volume was then scrutinised by the Prophet's companions and given to Hafsah, the Prophet's later wife, for safe-keeping and reference.

Meanwhile, Islam had spread beyond Arabia. Some 12 years later, during the caliphate of Othman, the Caliph learnt that non-Arabs in other territories were reading and reciting the Qur'an, which is in Arabic, with different accent and pronunciation. Taking present day differences in pronunciation as an example, we see Australians pronounce certain English words differently from the English; "Day" for instance, is pronounced as "dai" by the Australians.

Caliph Othman, who was another close companion of the Prophet, acted swiftly to prevent the differences in pronunciation and accent from getting wider. After consulting with leading authorities, he formed a committee comprising the former scribes of the Qur'an, including the celebrated Zayd bin Thabit, to produce a standard copy for use by people of other races so that they would read the Qur'an with the same accent and pronunciation as that made by the man who received it — Prophet Muhammad.

This was done by inserting "accent" or "vowel" markings to the Arabic letters so that a Muslim of any race from any country and of any educational level would be able to read the Qur'an with the same correct accent and pronunciation even though he may not speak or understand the Arabic language. The standard volume was used as a prototype in making a number of copies.

These accent-marked copies of the Qur'an were then sent to all the principal cities, including Mecca, Medina, Kufa, Basrah and Damascus, for copies to be made.

Caliph Othman ordered all the earlier copies which did not have the accent markings to be recalled and burnt. Because the Qur'an is a sacred book, the copies were burnt and not simply discarded in a dumping ground. Even today, a Muslim would dispose of a worn out copy of the Qur'an by burning it, instead of tossing it into the rubbish bin. In fact, the Qur'an is so revered that no Muslim would put a copy of the Qur'an under his chair or bring it into the toilet.

Some of those earlier copies escaped destruction and can be seen in the museums of some Muslim countries, including in the Topkapi Palace Museum of Turkey. Today's copies of the Qur'an are exactly the same as the accent-marked copy initiated by Caliph Othman. Likewise, the accent-marked copy is exactly the same as the first copy initiated by the Prophet; the only difference is that the first copy had no accent markings. As for the text, today's copies have exactly the same text as the first copy — the one seen by the Prophet himself. Even the Arabs who are fluent in Arabic use the same accent-marked Qur'an.

God says that the Qur'an is "a Guide, a Mercy and Glad Tidings to Muslims." (16:89) As such, the Qur'an is respected and held in high esteem by Muslims.

MEMORISING GOD'S WORDS

The Qur'an is in Arabic as revealed to Prophet Muhammad. Though in Arabic script, non-Arab Muslims have learnt to read it and committed large portions of it to memory. God says: "We have indeed made the Qur'an easy to remember ..." (54:17) This is evident from the time when Prophet Muhammad asked the Revelations that came to him to be memorised, and indeed each and every verse of the Qur'an was memorised by his companions.

Memorising some chapters of the Qur'an is necessary because Muslims recite them during the *solat* (Islamic prayers). Muslims also read the Qur'an whenever they have the time, especially after their *solat*. The vowel markings in the Qur'an have made it easier for non-Arabs to read the Qur'an with correct pronunciation.

Muslims recite chapters of the Qur'an, often en masse, when they attend funerals and anniversary celebrations like birthdays.

Even religious lectures begin with the recital of some Qur'anic verses relevant to the theme of the lecture. Muslims also read the Qur'an during each night of the fasting month of Ramadan, whether at the mosque or at home, and complete reading the whole Qur'an by the end of the month. They do this during the fasting month as part of their *ibadah* (acts of good deeds) because the Qur'an was first revealed to Prophet Muhammad in this very month, 17 Ramadan to be exact, and Muslims all over the world commemorate this day, called "Nuzul Al-Qur'an", by reading the Qur'an. God says: "Ramadan is the month in which the Qur'an was sent down, a guidance for mankind." (2:185) Most importantly, every word in the Qur'an is from God, not from human composition, thus, the love for memorising God's Words.

Many Muslims in the world, including young people, are able to recite the whole Qur'an without looking at the text. A person who has memorised the whole Qur'an is called a *hafiz*.

A *hafiz* is highly respected in the Muslim community as he has not only committed the whole Qur'an to memory but is also well-versed in *tajwid* (rules of Qur'anic recitation) and trained in vocalisation. A *hafiz* usually gets his training from a *madrasah*, a *hafiz*-training centre or other Islamic institutions.

A would-be *hafiz* is tested in various disciplines apart from Qur'anic knowledge. For instance, the candidate would be asked to continue reciting a passage taken randomly from the Qur'an. As he does not know which passage would be chosen, he must know the whole Qur'anic text in order to respond to the test. In some other tests, a would-be *hafiz* might be asked to recite verses containing a specific word or phrase. Only when he passes all these disciplines would he receive the title of "Hafiz".

Reading the Qur'an is a *barakah* (blessing), so is listening to it. Prophet Muhammad said: "The person whose recitation and voice is most beautiful is one who, when you hear him recite, you can feel that he fears God." Putting the teachings they read from the Qur'an into practice brings greater blessing. "Those who listen to the Word (the Qur'an) and follow the best meaning in it; those are the ones whom God has guided." (39:18)

Also, God Himself instructs: "When the Qur'an is read, listen to it with respect and attention." (7:204) Indeed Muslims do so.

TRANSLATIONS OF THE QUR'AN

Most non-Arab Muslims who do not know Arabic, understand the text by reading the translation of it in the language they know. Translations are available in many global languages. Well-known translated works in English, for instance, are those by Leopold Weiss (Muhammad Asad), a German convert; Muhammad Marmaduke Pickthall, a British convert; and Abdullah Yusuf Ali, a Muslim scholar from India who excelled in English whilst at Oxford University. Many of these translated works place the Arabic text adjacent to the English translation for easy reference.

The Qur'an is a Qur'an only when it is in Arabic, the original language by which it was revealed to Prophet Muhammad and recorded in print and available to anyone. If a translation is totally in English or in a language other than Arabic, that volume is not the Qur'an but a translation or interpretation. Hence, all those verses quoted in the non-Arabic language, strictly speaking, are not the Words of Allah, though for ease of communication, Muslim writers, including the author of this book, use such indicators as "The Qur'an says" and "God says".

6 🕌 SPIRITUAL NOURISHMENT

The *solat* (Islamic prayers) is the most important spiritual activity of a Muslim's life. Its prime objective is to create consciousness and awareness of and closeness to God. The *solat* involves total concentration of the mind and presence of heart.

"*Solat* at fixed times is prescribed for the believers." (4:102) Just as the physical body requires nourishment at several points in the day for sustenance, growth and strength, the *solat* is prescribed to be performed five times a day at appointed periods for spiritual benefit and development (20:130). (See Appendix D for the names of the *solat* and the times they are to be performed.)

There are three other activities that have significant bearings to the *solat*. They are the *azan* (prayer call), the *wudhu* (ablution or purification before the *solat* using clean water) and the *do'a* (supplication).

THE PRAYER CALL

The *azan* announces the entry point of each of the five *solat* of the day. The human voice is used to announce the time for the *solat* because the *azan* acts as the international anthem of the *ummah*, the global community of Muslims.

The *azan* comprises the cardinal points of Islam and the *Shahadah*, the Testimony of Faith, and an invitation to come "to success", a noble invitation with a deep meaning harmonising the well-being of both this world and the next. The *azan* is called out in Arabic. Translated, it goes thus:

- God is Great. (4 times)
- I bear witness that there is none worthy of worship except God. (2 times)

- I bear witness that Muhammad is the Messenger of God. (2 times)
- Come to *solat*. (2 times)
- Come to success. (2 times)
- God is Great. (2 times)
- There is none worthy of worship except God. (1 time)

The entry point of each of the *solat* changes slightly in progressive paces (according to the pace of the sun). A Muslim begins his *solat* anytime after the entry point of the *solat* and not before it. Hence, to hear the *azan* is important.

In Muslim countries, the *azan*, apart from being heard from loudspeakers placed atop minarets of mosques, is also made over the radio and television. In Singapore, it is broadcast over the Malay radio station. Copies of the *solat* timetable are also available, separately on cards or printed on the calendar. So, if one does not hear the *azan*, one can refer to the timetable to ascertain the time for the *solat*.

The *azan* is highly respected by Muslims. When a Muslim hears the *azan*, he responds to it silently with a "reply", phrase by phrase. If he enters the mosque when the *azan* is being called out, he keeps standing as a mark of respect for the *azan* until it ends.

The person who calls out the *azan* is the *muezzin*. The first person who was given the honour of calling out the *azan* was not a rich and renowned Arab, but a poor black African named Bilal. He was a slave of a rich pagan household who secretly embraced Islam. As his masters horribly tortured him for becoming a Muslim, Abu Bakar, a companion of the Prophet, bought the tortured slave and set him free. He became a staunch follower of Islam, and the Prophet picked him to be the first *muezzin* in Islamic history.

Any Muslim with a clear and loud voice can be the *muezzin*. The sound of the *azan* is augmented by the skill of the person who recites it — the more melodious, harmonious and clear the voice, the more powerful and captivating the *azan* is.

THE ABLUTION

The *wudhu* (ablution) is undertaken to keep oneself pure in mind, body and soul in preparation for the *solat*. Keeping oneself physically clean and spiritually pure at all times is the main thrust in Islam. "God loves those who keep themselves pure and clean." (2:222)

Prophet Muhammad said:

- "Purify yourself because Islam is a religion of purity."
- "The key of the *solat* is purification (through the *wudhu*)."
- "The key to Paradise is the *solat* and that to the *solat* is ablution."

God instituted the *wudhu* (5:7) as a prelude to the *solat*. The Prophet showed his followers how to perform the *wudhu* and this helped all Muslims throughout the ages to perform it in exactly the same way as he did. The *wudhu* is performed, first, by washing the hands up to the wrists, then the mouth, nostrils and face, then the arms up to the elbows; wetting the head above the forehead (this part of the head is often clean, hence no thorough washing is required); washing the ears (inside and outside), then the neck (all round), and finally, the feet up to the ankles.

At each *wudhu* undertaking, the Muslim washes all these parts of his body three times consecutively for thoroughness, uttering some short prayer statements as he washes them. Most importantly, apart from physical cleanliness, the *wudhu* serves to purify him spiritually. The Prophet said: "He who performs his *wudhu* well purifies his soul." Thus, when approaching God (for the *solat*), the Muslim is already in the best state of spiritual preparedness.

The *wudhu* also has hygienic and therapeutic values. It cleans and soothes the vital areas of the body such as the face, ears, nostrils, neck, forehead, arms and legs. Done five times a day, it softens the cleansed areas and prevents premature wrinkling and refreshes the person.

Islam teaches a person to be clean and pure in mind, body and soul at all times, including in all his intentions and actions.

THE PRAYER

The *solat* is not a mere prayer but a highly formalised way of communication with God. There is a difference between the *solat* and a *do'a*, which is a spontaneous activity that can be said anytime, often to beseech God for some favours, but the *solat* is prescribed and performed at appointed periods of the day (as mentioned in the Qur'an at 9:116; 20:130 and 30:17–18). (See Appendix E for the difference in detail.)

God mentions the *solat* in numerous ways in the Qur'an, such as:

- "Seek the help (of God) with patient perseverance and the *solat*." (2:153)
- "Perform the *solat* and give alms." (2:43)
- "… establish regular *solat*, enjoin what is just, and forbid what is wrong, and bear with constancy whatever may befall you …" (31:13–19)

God thus asks the Muslim to perform not only the *solat* but other righteous acts as well, in tandem.

While, in the Qur'an, God emphasises the importance of the *solat*, Prophet Muhammad taught and demonstrated the various postures and recitations by performing the *solat* together with his followers. Thus, the way Muslims perform the *solat* today is exactly the same as that performed by the Prophet.

The *solat* is performed individually or in a group of two or more persons at home, in the mosque, or anywhere else as long as the place is clean and has no distraction. An individual *solat* can be performed in a few minutes. However there is more merit in performing the *solat* in a group than alone and the larger the group, the more the merit. Therefore, when a male member of a family, be he the father or son, performs the *solat* at home, it would be more meritorious if he invites the other members of the family to perform the *solat* together with him. In the mosque, he performs the *solat* together with other Muslims.

Muslims perform the *solat* facing towards the Ka'aba in Mecca. The *solat* consists of *raka'at* (units). Each unit comprises a set of postures from standing (for attentiveness), bowing (for respect), prostrating (for humility) and sitting (for togetherness). During each posture, the Muslim recites certain phrases and Qur'anic verses softly under his breath, all in the language of the Qur'an — Arabic. In concluding the *solat*, the Muslim says a *do'a* with his arms raised to elbow-level and hands cupped, seeking God's blessings in earnest humility.

Menstruating women are exempted from the *solat* and, unlike fasting, they need not make up for all the missed *solat* when the menstruation period is over.

Apart from the five obligatory *solat*, there are many voluntary *solat*, the most common being those performed before and after each of the main *solat*.

The Muslim who performs the *solat* with full concentration gets absorbed mentally, physically and spiritually in his communication with God and in turn receives peace, relaxation and rejuvenation from his daily work routine. It also helps to regularise his daily activities and promotes positive values like punctuality, discipline and endeavour.

THE SUPPLICATION

Apart from the *solat*, a Muslim is also strongly encouraged to call upon God to seek His blessings and guidance. This is the *do'a* (supplication).

While the *solat* is personal and cannot be performed for the benefit of other people, a *do'a* can be offered to seek God's help for one's own self or others. Examples of a *do'a* include someone asking God to give him strength in carrying out certain responsibilities, to show him guidance in making a complicated decision, to forgive him or others for a certain unrighteous act committed, and to bless him or others for a safe journey during a travel trip. The Muslim is also encouraged to say a *do'a* for someone who is sick, beseeching God to help him get well soon.

A *do'a* cannot be carried out for anything that is un-Islamic, like asking God to curse someone or asking God to help him win a lottery.

When offering the *do'a*, the supplicant lifts both his hands up to about chest level with open palms. He does this because he is asking his Creator for His blessings, help, guidance and mercy. The supplicant would then place his palms over his face with hope and thanks. This act is the highest form of humility and humbleness before God, just like prostrating during the *solat*.

The Muslim usually offers a general *do'a* after the *solat* as this is the purest moment of his time, having just completed the *solat* and still maintaining the *wudhu*, a desirable time to seek God's blessings and guidance.

Islam holds that a person's *do'a* reaches God without the need for intermediaries. As such, Muslims communicate with God directly without the necessity of a priest or any middleman to relay their prayer, supplication or repentance to God. Contact with God is personal, direct and mental. God assures the believer that He listens to his *do'a*. "I listen to the *do'a* of every supplicant when he calls on Me..." (2:186)

The Muslim is also aware that it does not mean that every *do'a* he makes will be answered according to what he wants. Only God knows best what is good for the individual supplicant and for the whole community. The Muslim also knows that if his *do'a* does not seem to be answered directly or quickly, it is because things happen not according to the will of the supplicant but according to the will of God. Indeed, if everyone got all he asked for, there would be chaos and confusion in the world. Therefore, God, in His wisdom and perfect knowledge of all our real needs, responds to a *do'a* in various subtle ways.

7 🕌 HOUSE OF GOD

"None is worthy of worship except God" is Islam's principle which is enshrined in the "Al-Fatiha", the opening chapter of the Qur'an. Islam teaches Muslims to worship God by following His commands and practising Islamic righteousness. One of the commands of God is for Muslims to perform the *solat*. They can perform it at home or anywhere, but performing the *solat* in the mosque is meritorious.

THE MOSQUE

A *masjid* (mosque) is a "House of God", meaning it is a place where Muslims gather to perform the *solat,* which is said in Arabic.

Mosques around the world have a wide diversity of architectural styles, from imposing domes and slender minarets to simple, plain-looking buildings. However, the internal features are more important.

As the *solat* consists of Qur'anic recitations and a set of body postures that include standing, bowing, prostrating and sitting, the prayer halls in the mosque are open spaces without benches or chairs. In modern times, the floor is carpeted wall to wall.

People form straight rows one after another facing the *qibla* (direction of the Ka'aba in Mecca), leaving sufficient space between the rows for prostrating.

Another important feature of the mosque is the *mihrab* (niche) on the front wall, known as the *qibla* wall. This wall indicates the direction of Mecca. People form rows parallel to this wall, facing it. (In hotel rooms in Malaysia and in other Muslim countries, the *qibla* is indicated by an arrow somewhere in the room, often painted on the ceiling or in drawers to aid Muslim guests in their performance of their *solat*. These days travellers often carry a *qibla* compass for this purpose. In Muslim homes, the direction is easily established with this compass.)

The *imam* (*solat* leader) takes his position just in front of the *mihrab* during the *solat*. People stand in rows behind the *imam* who himself faces the *qibla* during the *solat*.

Another feature of the mosque is the *mimbar* (stepped pulpit) where the *imam* stands when delivering the *khutbah* (sermon). The sermon is delivered only for the Friday, Eid ul-Fitri (Festival of Charity) and Eid ul-Adha (Festival of Sacrifice) *solat*. In Singapore, the sermon for each week is prepared by the Islamic Religious Council of Singapore (Muis) and all mosques use the same script for uniformity of the subject matter covered. The message in the sermon is about moral and ethical teachings of Islam related to current social happenings like drug abuses and divorces among youths. The sermon can be delivered in any language. In Singapore, sermons are delivered predominantly in Malay. However, because of the increasing number of converts to Islam, English is used for the sermon in some mosques. Other countries use their own languages for the sermon.

Since free-mixing of the sexes is not allowed in the mosque, the building usually has separate ablution areas and prayer halls for males and females.

There are no statues, paintings or pictures in the prayer halls as these are forbidden in Islam. For aesthetic beauty, the higher parts of the walls are adorned with Qur'anic verses, often in calligraphic form.

Since the beginning of Islam, the mosque has also been a place for learning and charitable work. Therefore, a mosque building may include a meeting room and a *madrasah* (religious school for children and young people) or rooms for religious classes for adults. Religious lectures by visiting Islamic scholars may also be held in the prayer halls before or after the main *solat*. During the fasting month of Ramadan, mosques serve food for those breaking fast in the mosque.

PRAYERS IN THE MOSQUE

Islam encourages Muslims to perform the *solat* together with other Muslims in a congregation in the "House of God" (mosque), firstly, because of the purity of the place as people are there for just one intention — to worship God, and not take it as a place for family gathering or merry-making or to meet one's boyfriend or girlfriend; secondly, so that they can meet other Muslims and build rapport and togetherness through wholesome conversation. As such, the mosque is the most suitable and desired place for performing the *solat* as well as for holding any Islamic activities. God says: "The mosques of God shall be visited and used ..." (9:18)

The following types of *solat* are performed in the mosque:

- the five daily obligatory *solat*.
- the *Juma'ah* (Friday) *solat* which is also obligatory. This *solat* takes the place of the *zohor* (early afternoon) *solat*.
- the *terawih solat*. This is the night-time *solat* performed throughout the fasting month of Ramadan after the *ishak* or night *solat*.
- the Eid ul-Fitri (Festival of Charity) *solat*.
- the Eid ul-Adha (Festival of Sacrifice) *solat*.
- the *jenazah* (funeral) *solat*.
- various voluntary *solat*. The voluntary *solat* is performed individually, not in a congregation.

The *solat* performed in a congregation are led by the *imam*. The *imam* is not a priest as there is no priesthood in Islam. He is an ordinary but righteous and respectable man who is well versed in Qur'anic knowledge. He may be a volunteer or employed by the mosque.

A typical scene in the prayer hall of a mosque, say, for the Friday *solat*, would be as follows:

- People enter the *solat* hall after taking the *wudhu* at the ablution area. They perform a voluntary *solat* of greeting and respect for the mosque. After completing it, they sit, waiting for the *azan*. They occupy the time by reading the Qur'an, meditation or saying the *zikir* (reciting the names of God), all silently so as not to disturb the neighbours.
- When the *azan* is heard over the public address system, everyone in the premises of the mosque (inside and outside the mosque) respond to it phrase by phrase under their breath. Those who enter the hall now do not sit but remain standing as a mark of respect for the *azan*, responding to it as the others.
- Immediately after the *azan*, everyone fills gaps left in the rows between each of those already there, and then performs another voluntary *solat*. This is a prelude *solat*, performed

before the main *solat*, whether it is the Friday *solat* or any of the five obligatory *solat*.

- Soon after, the *imam*, after he has performed his voluntary *solat*, goes to the *mimbar* and delivers the sermon. The Friday *solat* and the *solat* for Eid ul-Fitri and Eid ul-Adha include sermons. There are no sermons for the five obligatory *solat*.
- After the sermon, the *iqamah* (second *azan*) is called out, and now every person quickly gets himself organised in the proper main *solat* formation — standing very close to one another row after row behind the *imam*. Any gaps in the rows are quickly filled up so that everyone stands shoulder to shoulder in straight rows.
- The *imam* leads the congregation for the *solat* — the Friday *solat* consists of two *raka'at* (units).
- At the end of the *solat*, the *imam* offers a *do'a* (supplication) aloud. This is a collective *do'a*, with everyone in the congregation listening with raised open palms and responding with *"ameen"* (amen). The *do'a* seeks God's blessings for the Prophet, the Muslim community and the country.
- After offering the general *do'a*, a third voluntary *solat* is performed to conclude the session. Following the *Sunnah*, no voluntary *solat* is performed after the *asar* (late afternoon) *solat*.
- People may leave the mosque after this *solat*.

A Muslim does not "belong" to any one particular mosque but to all mosques. This allows him to perform his *solat* in any mosque as is convenient to him from his home or workplace.

8 🕌 PILGRIMS' PARADISE

Mecca and Medina are Islam's most sacred cities where Muslims of various nationalities and cultures from all over the world converge to fulfil their spiritual obligations.

The Grand Mosque in Mecca and the Prophet's Mosque in Medina are the magnets that attract the largest congregation in the world at every *solat* of the day, year in and year out.

The two cities are modern and cosmopolitan, yet they are completely Islamic. In keeping with their image of being the holiest cities in Islam, places like nightclubs (where males and females mix freely) and public swimming pools or health clubs (where the body is exposed) are not operated. Government authorities also make sure that violence and immorality are censored all round.

Mecca and Medina, strictly off-limits to non-Muslims, provide a refuge for Muslims who want to experience Islam in its most pristine and complete form, without the distraction of tourists and people of non-Islamic lifestyles. Here, Muslims from all over the world are able to practise the life pattern of Islam without any compromise.

MECCA
Makkah al-Mukarramah (Makkah the Blessed or Ennobled), often spelt as "Mecca", is well known for two main reasons: one, it is the birthplace of Islam and its last Prophet, Prophet Muhammad; and two, it contains the world-famous Ka'aba towards which Muslims around the world face when performing their *solat*.

Since the 1980s, some 2.5 million pilgrims have been converging on Mecca annually for the Haj, the major pilgrimage, in Zulhijjah, the 12th month of the Muslim calendar, and millions more for the Umrah, the minor pilgrimage, in the other 11 months of the year.

Mecca is described as a sacred city of peace and security in the Qur'an (90:1–3 and 95:3). The whole Meccan area is called "*Haram*", a word which means both sacred and forbidden — "forbidden from committing anything undesirable, detested or profane". The sacredness of Mecca is further enhanced by the rules of "right conduct" which are to be observed by Muslims performing the pilgrimage. No one should gossip, use abusive words or quarrel. God says: "Whoever determines the performance of the pilgrimage therein, there shall be no foul speech, nor abusing, nor disputing." (2:197) Also, pilgrims should not beg, kill any animal, or even cut a tree inside this forbidden zone.

Mecca only became a settlement during the time of Prophet Abraham, as a consequence of his leaving his wife, Hagar, in the desert valley of Mecca. Today, Mecca has numerous schools and institutions of higher learning. It has modern roads and highways linking the other cities of the country. There are hospitals and first-class hotels as well as other advanced facilities. In Mecca, all the roads lead to Masjidil Haram — the pulsating heart of Mecca.

THE GRAND MOSQUE

Masjidil Haram (Sacred Mosque), which is often referred to as the Grand Mosque, contains the Ka'aba, the cube-like structure located in the middle of its quadrangle. This is the only mosque in the world where the *saf* (prayer rows) is circular instead of straight. This is because of the proximity of the people standing shoulder to shoulder (in circular rows) around the Ka'aba which is the point towards which Muslims in that mosque and around the world face when performing their *solat*.

The mosque is never closed. At any time of the day or night, even at two or three o'clock in the morning, there are crowds of people performing the *tawaf* (going round the Ka'aba seven times in an anti-clockwise direction) or the *solat* or reading the Qur'an.

Masjidil Haram is also famous for the Black Stone embedded in the wall of the Ka'aba, the Well of Zamzam and the hillocks, Safa and Marwa. While the Ka'aba is associated with four of Islam's prophets, the well and the hillocks, located within the mosque premises, are associated with Hagar, the second wife of Prophet Abraham, and their son, Ishmael.

The Ka'aba

The Ka'aba is covered with a black silken cloth, called *kiswa*, with the *Shahadah* (Testimony of Faith) outlined in the weave of the fabric. Towards the upper end runs a gold embroidered band covered with Qur'anic verses.

God instructs Muslims to face towards the Ka'aba when performing their *solat* as a symbol of unity in worship: "(O Muslims), wheresoever you may be, turn your faces towards it (during the *solat*)." (2:144)

The Ka'aba is also where the *tawaf* is performed by the pilgrims. It is "the first House (of worship) appointed for mankind" (3:96). A Hadith says that the person who laid the foundation of the "House" and the first person to pray at the spot was Prophet Adam, father of mankind and Islam's first prophet.

Numerous generations later, Prophet Abraham and his son, Ishmael, built the Ka'aba for people to walk around it as a devotional act in the worship of the One God. God says: "Abraham and Ishmael raised the foundation of the House with a prayer." (2:127) Again God says: "We made the House a place of assembly for men and a place of safety... and We covenanted with Abraham and Ishmael that they should sanctify My House for those who go around it, or use it as a retreat or prostrate themselves (towards it during the *solat*)." (2:125)

At least four of Islam's great prophets are associated with the Ka'aba. They are:

- The first prophet, Prophet Adam, who laid the foundation of the Ka'aba and prayed there.

- Prophet Abraham who built the Ka'aba as a cube-like structure (upon receiving God's instructions through the Archangel Gabriel) and called the faithful to go round it as an act of piety.

- Prophet Ishmael, the son of Prophet Abraham, who in his youth, helped his father build the Ka'aba, and when he became a prophet, continued the teachings of his father, including going round the Ka'aba as an act of piety.

- Prophet Muhammad, who:
  1. Before his prophethood and because of his shining character, was asked by the elders to assist in placing the

Black Stone back in the same corner of the Ka'aba from where it was removed for renovation.

2. When he became a prophet, he re-established the Ka'aba as a place of worship of the One God by removing the numerous idols placed there by the pagans.
3. Himself performed the *tawaf*.
4. Upon receiving God's Revelation, asked Muslims to face towards the Ka'aba during their *solat*.

In modern times, Muslims have been coming to the "House" (the Ka'aba) for the Haj and the Umrah in increasing numbers, fulfilling the Qur'anic prediction: "the House that is much frequented." (52:4)

The Black Stone

This stone, called "*Hajar ul-Aswad*", is oval in shape and about 30 centimetres long and 25 centimetres wide. Embedded in massive silver and set at one of the four corners of the Ka'aba about 1.2 metres from the ground, it is convenient for pilgrims to kiss it.

Pilgrims are encouraged to kiss the Black Stone, only if they are able to, as the wave of pilgrims encircling the Ka'aba day and night is thick and endless. The Black Stone was touched and even kissed by Prophet Muhammad. It was also touched by two earlier prophets — Prophet Abraham and his son, Prophet Ishmael. The kissing thus enables Muslims to be spiritually in "touch" with these three prophets of God and with all pilgrims throughout the ages.

The Well of Zamzam and Hillocks Safa and Marwa

Hagar was asked to stay at this (once deserted) spot by her husband, Prophet Abraham. Having finished the provision of water she had, she began to look for water. She placed her baby, Ishmael, under a shade, and earnestly praying to God for His intervention, she frantically ran between Safa and Marwa to get a view of the area from the top of the hillocks to see if there was any caravan passing by to get help. Seeing none, she returned to her baby and to her amazement she saw water — the Zamzam water — miraculously issuing out of the earth near the infant.

Today, the actual well, although quite close to the Ka'aba, is not visible from any part of the mosque. The well, facilitated by a modern piping system, is housed in an underground chamber to provide space for pilgrms to perform the *tawaf* and the *solat* at the quadrangle of the mosque.

The water from the well is ice-cold and available free of charge from numerous huge dispensers placed along the corridors of the mosque. Disposable plastic cups are replaced and the dispensers filled very regularly by hundreds of hardworking workers.

The Zamzam water, the result of God's response to Hagar's earnest *do'a*, has continued to flow incessantly right to this day, quenching the thirst of Hagar, Prophet Abraham, Prophet Ishmael, Prophet Muhammad and millions upon millions of pilgrims since then. No other water in the world has reached as far and wide on earth as the Zamzam water. Today pilgrims undertaking the Haj and Umrah not only drink the water as much as they like and at any time of the day or night during the pilgrimage, but also bring it back home in special containers.

MEDINA

Madinah Al-Munawwarah (Madinah the Enlightened or Radiant), often spelt as "Medina", is located about 500 kilometres from, and exactly north of, Mecca.

Although it is not a requirement of the Haj or Umrah pilgrims to visit Medina, no pilgrim would miss the opportunity to visit this city before or after their pilgrimage in Mecca. Visiting Medina is a journey of love for the Prophet.

Medina became the magnet for Islam from the time of Prophet Muhammad's migration (*Hijrah*) in the year 622, then an oasis town called Yathrib. Yathrib soon became known as Medinatul Nabi (City of the Prophet) or simply Medina. The city became the educational centre and the capital of Islam at the time of the Prophet and three of the four caliphs after the Prophet.

Apart from the Prophet's Mosque, pilgrims to Medina would earnestly visit two other mosques — Masjid Quba and Masjid Qiblatain — and perform at least one *solat* in each of these mosques for the very special reason that the Prophet himself had tarried and performed his *solat* there.

The Quba Mosque, situated about four kilometres outside Medina, was the first mosque in Islam built with the hands of Prophet Muhammad. When the persecution of the Prophet became very intense in Mecca, he and his companion, Abu Bakar, left Mecca for Medina. Before they reached Medina, they stayed in Quba for a few days and it was during this time that the Prophet built this mosque upon receiving a Revelation from God. Masjid Quba has been highly spoken of in the Qur'an as Masjid At-Taqwa, a mosque founded on piety (9:104).

The Qiblatain Mosque was where Prophet Muhammad received the Revelation to face towards the Ka'aba when performing the *solat*. The Revelation came when the Prophet and other Muslims were praying together, facing the Al-Aqsa Mosque in Jerusalem, the third holiest mosque in Islam. With help from the Archangel Gabriel who delivered the instruction, the Prophet at once changed his direction towards the Ka'aba.

Visitors would also take every opportunity to visit two significant cemeteries to offer their *do'a*. These are the Uhud and Baqi Cemeteries, famous in Islamic history because the former was where Hamza, the Prophet's uncle who was with him throughout his difficult mission to deliver the Message of Islam, was buried, and the latter was where more than 1,000 companions of the Prophet were buried.

Indeed a visit to Medina revives in the heart of a Muslim the memories of the Prophet's struggles and accomplishments of his mission of delivering the Message of Islam. Visitors to Medina would spend most of their time performing the obligatory and voluntary *solat* in the Prophet's Mosque, the second holiest mosque in Islam.

THE PROPHET'S MOSQUE

When the Prophet first came to Medina upon his migration from Mecca, he built a mosque, now called Masjid Nabawi (Mosque of the Prophet) near his home. Ten years later, the Prophet performed the Haj in Mecca. Three months after his return from the Farewell Pilgrimage, the Prophet passed away, on 8 June 632. According to his own wishes, he was buried under the earthen floor of the very same room of his little house.

Tomb of Prophet Muhammad

When Masjid Nabawi was expanded, the chamber where the Prophet was buried became enclosed at one end of the mosque building. The chamber, known as *"Maqam Rasulullah"* ("Tomb of Prophet

Muhammad"), is enclosed to prevent people from going near it and upsetting the peace and quiet of the area. People offer their *do'a* from outside the grilled chamber.

Garden in Paradise
A very important section of Masjid Nabawi is the *"Raudhah al-Jannah"*, a special *solat* area adjacent to the Prophet's tomb. The section, which is likened to a Garden in Paradise, is always packed with people performing voluntary and obligatory *solat* to receive divine blessings.

Masjid Nabawi is the second largest mosque next to Masjidil Haram. It is fully air-conditioned with a number of high-tech features. For instance, in the evenings, its numerous huge domes are retracted electronically to provide circulation of fresh air and a good view of the clear night sky.

9 ⌂ CELEBRATORY OCCASIONS

Muslims base all their festivals and commemorative events on the Islamic calendar, known as the Hijrah calendar. Since these are religious events, they are celebrated without extravagance and pompous merry-making. All start with prayers.

The Hijrah calendar is lunar-based, therefore the celebration of Muslim festivals and events begin in the evening, after sunset, at the time of the *maghrib solat*, not at midnight. For instance, the celebration of Zikral Hijrah (Muslim New Year) begins with special prayers at the mosques, first with the year-ending *do'a* just before the *maghrib solat*, and then with the new-year *do'a* after the *maghrib solat*. Activities, such as religious lectures, quizzes for students and any other Islamically appropriate events organised for the celebration of the Muslim New Year, are held when the day begins.

Other celebratory occasions include the Birthday of Prophet Muhammad, Eid ul-Fitri (Festival of Charity) and Eid ul-Adha (Festival of Sacrifice). (See Appendix F for the names of the months and the main events celebrated by Muslims.)

THE ISLAMIC CALENDAR

The Islamic or Hijrah calendar started from the event known as the "*Hijrah*" (migration of Prophet Muhammad from Mecca to Medina). The *Hijrah* took place on 2 July in the year 622 of the Gregorian calendar. It not only denotes the triumph, success and progress of Islam, but also marks the founding of the brotherhood of Islam.

The Hijrah calendar is based on the movement of the moon. It takes an average of 29.5 days for the moon to go through the phases in one (Gregorian) month. Thus, a lunar year has only 354 days, shorter than the solar year by approximately 11 days. Also, since the Hijrah months are intended to rotate over the Gregorian calendar, the "lost" days are not "made up" to form a leap year on the English calendar. Due to this special feature, Eid ul-Fitri, for example, is celebrated 11 days earlier each year.

Again, taking Eid ul-Fitri as an example, the Hijrah calendar allows this festival to rotate over all the months of the Gregorian calendar. Thus, Eid ul-Fitri falls twice or thrice in every month of the English calendar as it advances over a 33-year cycle before coming near to the same point again. For example, in recent years, Eid ul-Fitri fell three times in the month of July, namely, 28 July 2014, 17 July 2015 and 6 July 2016; and this year (2017), it fell on 25 June, advancing by 11 days each year.

The advantage of the Hijrah calendar is that any Islamic festival or event takes place in every season of the solar calendar. For instance, Muslims will have the experience of fasting in the month of Ramadan in all the 12 months of the solar calendar. The Hijrah calendar hence allows variety and removes the monotony of people in any one country celebrating any festival or going through any religious event in the same season of the solar calendar year in and year out forever.

The Muslim year is differentiated from the English year with a "H" for Hijrah. For example, the start of the Muslim New Year of 1438H, which in 2016 coincided with 2 October, means that the Hijrah of Prophet Muhammad took place 1,438 (lunar) years ago on the Hijrah calendar.

Muslims celebrate Islamic New Year, called Zikral Hijrah, with special prayers, especially in mosques and as a national event in Muslim countries. The Islamic New Year is the first day of Muharram, which is the first of the 12 months in the Islamic lunar calendar.

ISLAMIC PILGRIMAGES: HAJ AND UMRAH

The Haj, undertaken for one's self-renewal and devotion to God, is the fifth of the Five Pillars of Islam. It is obligatory for every Muslim adult who is financially able and physically fit to perform the Haj once in his or her lifetime. The Umrah (minor pilgrimage) is not obligatory. However, Haj pilgrims also undertake the Umrah during the same trip. God tells Muslims to "accomplish the Haj and the Umrah in the service of God" (2:196).

The Haj is held once a year in Zulhijjah, the 12th month of the Muslim calendar. The Umrah, on the other hand, can be performed at any time of the year outside the Haj season. A Muslim can take either the Haj or the Umrah trip first, but only the Haj fulfils the requirement of the fifth Pillar of Islam. The Umrah is voluntary.

During the Haj, a pilgrim re-enacts the trials and tribulations of three personalities — Prophet Abraham, his second wife Hagar, and their son Ishmael.

The religious activities of the Haj are performed in Arafah, Muzdalifa, Mina and Mecca, while those of the Umrah are performed entirely in Mecca.

The main common features of both the Haj and the Umrah are the *ihram* and *tawaf*.

Ihram

When pilgrims from all over the world reach Mecca for the Haj or Umrah, every male pilgrim must have already put on a simple, two-piece unsewn white cotton cloth for the *ihram* (a state of devotion or consecration). His head is left bare and he wears no shoes but slippers, which are to be left outside the mosque. The female pilgrim wears any decent clothing that covers her body loosely from head to toe except the face and hands. Everyone now is equal in status and bent on achieving more piety. Only after performing certain rituals would the pilgrim wear normal Islamic clothing again.

Tawaf

This is the act of going round the Ka'aba seven times in an anti-clockwise direction. The conditions to observe for the *tawaf* are similar to those of the *solat*. For instance, people have to be in a state of purity by taking the *wudhu* first. The *tawaf* is the first act of the pilgrim upon arrival in Mecca and the final one before leaving it.

The exclusive features of the Haj are the *wukuf*, the *Rami Jamrah* and the *qurban*:

Wukuf

The *wukuf* is the presence of every Haj pilgrim in Arafah on 9 Zulhijjah. During the one-day *wukuf*, pilgrims stay in temporarily erected tents, spending their time reading the Qur'an, performing the obligatory and voluntary *solat* and listening to the Haj sermon. This is the zenith of the Haj.

Rami Jamrah

From Arafah, the pilgrims travel to Mina where they will stay for three days for the "stoning of Satan" ritual. Pebbles, picked up in Muzdalifa on the way to Mina, are thrown at the three *jamrahs* (stone structures representing Satan). This ritual is a re-enactment of the trial of Prophet Abraham and his son, Ishmael, a youth at this time. God, through the Archangel Gabriel, asked Prophet Abraham to sacrifice his son, the most valued "possession" of a father, as a test of his faith in God. Though extremely crestfallen, he obeyed God. Ishmael accepted his fate with equal obedience. (Note: Different prophets were tested of their faith and missions in different ways.)

As both father and son were walking towards where the three *jamrahs* now stand, Satan appeared, in human form, asking them to disobey what God had commanded them to do. Both father and son pelted stones at Satan to drive him away. Thus, the "stoning of Satan" ritual is symbolic of resistance to evil temptations. As this act is symbolic, only pebbles are used and not stones or other harmful objects.

Qurban

This is the ceremony of slaughtering of sheep or camel. The ritual is carried out in Mina at a designated place during the three days. This day, 10 Zulhijjah, is Eid ul-Adha. Although the *qurban* is encouraged in Islam for those who can afford it, God reminds Muslims: "It is not their meat or blood that reaches God. It is your piety that reaches Him." (22:37) The meat is deep-frozen by the Saudi authorities and donated to the poor and charitable organisations in other countries.

The exclusive feature of the Umrah is the *Sa'i*. This is the ritual where pilgrims walk briskly between Safa and Marwa, two hillocks about 400 metres apart. In modern times, these hillocks are housed within the compound of the Sacred Mosque. *Sa'i* is performed to acknowledge and commemorate the hardship experienced by Hagar, when she ran between these hillocks in search of water, after she had laid down her son, Ishmael, nearby.

More and more Muslims are performing the Haj today. Each year since the 1980s, some 2.5 million Muslims from all over the world, with diverse cultures, languages, background, ranks and status, converge on Mecca for this biggest multi-racial event in the world.

FESTIVAL OF SACRIFICE (EID UL-ADHA)
The full impact of Eid ul-Adha (Festival of Sacrifice), or Hari Raya Haji in Malay, is felt by those pilgrims who are performing the Haj. On that day, the pilgrims feel a mixture of happiness and sadness, happy because they have already fulfilled the requirements of the fifth Pillar of Islam and sad because they would soon be leaving Mecca.

The unique feature of Eid ul-Adha outside Mecca is the *qurban* (sacrifice) of sheep and cattle.

Qurban is carried out to commemorate the sacrifice undertaken by Prophet Abraham. His faith was tested by God who, through the Archangel Gabriel, asked him to sacrifice his son, Ishmael, who was a youth at the time. Though his love for his son was great, his love for God was greater. Ishmael's faith in God was no less intense and he readily consented to be sacrificed. But when Prophet Abraham placed the knife on his son's throat, a sheep appeared before them. At that moment, God (through the voice of Archangel Gabriel) told Prophet Abraham that the act of sacrifice of his son was only meant to test his faith. He need not sacrifice his son, but could offer the sheep instead as a gesture of thanksgiving for having overcome the ordeal.

Qurban is voluntary. Any male or female Muslim can make a *qurban* of any number of sheep. The *qurban* ceremony normally begins at about 10 o'clock in the morning after the Eid ul-Adha *solat* and lasts until the last sheep is slaughtered, skinned and the meat cut up into chunks and distributed.

Mosques and Muslim organisations holding the *qurban* ceremonies distribute the meat to the poor and needy and charitable homes. Those making the *qurban* may take home a portion of their sacrifice (a third of the meat) for distribution to their neighbours, relatives and friends.

Nowadays, many Singapore Muslims also hold the *qurban* in poor villages in Indonesia and China, executed through Muslim organisations.

Muslims celebrate Eid ul-Adha in a more personal way, because the main thrust in this celebration is the *qurban* — sacrifice and warding off of evil temptation — in both its physical and spiritual sense.

THE RAMADAN FAST

Ramadan is the ninth month of the Islamic calendar. During this month, Muslims all over the world are obliged to fast daily from dawn to dusk, refraining not only from food and water but also from smoking and marital sexual activity, as well as from any undesirable or negative thought, emotion and action including quarrelling, fighting, scolding and cursing.

Saum (fasting) is ordained by God. One of the main objectives of fasting is to learn to restrain oneself in any negative or challenging situation. God says: "O you who believe! Fasting is prescribed to you ... that you may learn self-restraint." (2:183)

In Singapore, Muslims fast for about 14 hours, from slightly before 5:00 am to 7:00 pm. The exact time of the commencement and termination of the fast depends on the sunrise and sunset time of the day, which varies slightly day by day. A Muslim cannot break his fast even a minute before the *maghrib azan* (the before-sunset prayer call).

A Muslim is exempted from fasting on those days when he is ill but he has to make up for the missed days after Ramadan at his own convenience. The mentally retarded, insane or the old and infirm need not make up. A Muslim woman, if she is menstruating or pregnant or has just given birth, need not fast but she has to repay the number of days missed any time before the next Ramadan. Fasting is not compulsory for children below the age of puberty.

A special late night Ramadan *solat* called "*terawih*" is conducted in all mosques. If there is no mosque nearby, the *terawih* can be performed in any big space or even in one's home with family members. This *solat* is performed immediately after the *ishak solat*.

Ramadan is the month when the Qur'an was first revealed to Prophet Muhammad. Therefore, Muslims often spend more time reading the Qur'an during this month. Mosques hold the *tadarus*, a Qur'an-reading session, during which those who can stay back after the *terawih solat* read one or two parts of the Qur'an each night until the whole Qur'an is completed before the end of Ramadan.

The last ten days of Ramadan is a very auspicious period. The *Lailatul Qadr* (Night of Power) occurs on one of these nights. According to the Prophet, this is a night that is better than 1,000 nights in its blessedness. Therefore, Muslims spend the night reading the Qur'an and performing voluntary *solat* in the mosques or at home. For this reason too, mosques and Muslim homes are lighted up until late into the night from the 21st night onwards.

Muslims are also more charity-conscious during Ramadan. They donate generously to help those in need. Every Muslim is also obliged to give to the poor the religious tithe called *zakat fitrah*. In Singapore, the money is collected by the Islamic Religious Council of Singapore (Muis) for distribution to the poor and needy.

Apart from providing health benefits by allowing the stomach to "rest", the Ramadan fast helps a Muslim in the uplifting of his spiritual values. Other benefits include the development of discipline, patience and determination, goodwill and compassion for the less fortunate, and the spirit of sacrifice, self-reliance and self-restraint, as well as physical health. Ramadan paves the way for togetherness and spiritual bonding among Muslims of the world.

The Prophet said: "Ramadan is a blessed month when God provides refuge for you and showers His mercy on you, cleanses you of your sins and grants your requests. Angels welcome you. Avail yourself, therefore, to all things good."

FESTIVAL OF CHARITY (EID UL-FITRI)

Eid ul-Fitri (Festival of Charity), or Hari Raya Aidil Fitri in Malay, is celebrated a day after the fasting month of Ramadan, on first Shawal.

Eid ul-Fitri is a time to strengthen friendship and fraternity and to seek forgiveness as a way to attain purity of the heart and soul. Malay Muslims, therefore, when meeting their relatives and friends during this period, say "*Maaf zahir dan batin*", a term used for seeking forgiveness, as they give the physical *salam* (like a handshake).

The most notable feature of this festival is the home visits. Normally, no invitation is required and even unknown guests of friends or relatives are welcomed to their homes. Non-Muslims may visit their Muslim friends on Eid ul-Fitri during which delicacies are served for all visitors. Muslims would be very happy to receive non-Muslim friends and neighbours to celebrate the occasion together.

Relatives and friends, ahead of Eid ul-Fitri, would send greetings for the occasion, via cards or Internet messages, by saying "*Eid Mubarak*", an international usage in Arabic, or "*Salam Aidil Fitri*" in Malay.

10 ☾CHARACTER BUILDING

Islam takes character building as an important aspect of its teachings on values and attitude. Prophet Muhammad's own personality is a good example to be emulated by Muslims. Even in his youth, the Prophet's pure character and his regard for truth and honesty was well known. The pagan Meccans who worshipped idols never called him a liar about the new *Deen* (the believers' way of life) he was introducing as coming from an Unseen God. He was still called *"Al-Amin"* (the trustworthy) and *"As-Saadiq"* (the truthful). They persecuted him because they were afraid that their age-old traditions would be eroded by Islam.

Values such as compassion and politeness, humility and modesty, patience and filial piety, respect, generosity and forgiveness are all universal virtues by which a person can "grow in purity" (91:9) and develop a character and personality that is pleasing to all.

VIRTUES

Virtues are so important in Islam that when a man asked Prophet Muhammad what Islam is and what *iman* (faith) is, the Prophet replied: "Islam is purity of speech and charity, and *iman* is patience and beneficence."

Numerous virtues are mentioned throughout the Qur'an. In Chapter 33, verse 35 alone, God mentions a number of them as shown in the table on the next page.

Quotation from the Qur'an (33:35):	The virtues referred to are:
"For Muslim men and women:	
who believe	(1) Faith, hope, and trust in God and in His benevolent government of the universe
who are devoted	(2) devotion and service in everyday life
who are true	(2) love and practice of truth in thought, intention, word and deed
who are patient and constant	(3) patience and constancy in suffering and in right endeavour
who humble themselves	(4) the avoidance of arrogance and superiority
who give charity	(5) helping the poor and the unfortunate in life, a special virtue arising out of the general duty of service to humanity
who fast	(6) self-denial in certain flesh of animals and food especially in the daylight hours of Ramadan, and generally in all bad appetites and desires
who guard their chastity	(8) purity in sex life, purity in motive, thought, word and deed
who engage much in God's praise	(9) constant attention to God's Message, and cultivation of the desire to get nearer to God
For them has God prepared forgiveness and a great reward." (33:35)	

The Qur'an and the Hadith are replete with instructions on Islamic virtues, such as:

- "He from whose injurious conduct his neighbours is not safe will not enter Paradise." (Hadith)
- "The noblest Muslim is he who is best in manners and character." (Hadith)
- "Every act of kindness is charity, and kindness includes meeting your brother with a cheerful face." (Hadith)
- "He does not belong to us (Muslims) who does not show kindness to children and respect to elders." (Hadith)
- "The one who visits the sick is like one who is in the fruit garden of Paradise until he returns." (Hadith)
- "A Muslim is he who avoids harming people with his tongue or hands." (Hadith)
- "Humility and courtesy are acts of piety." (Hadith)
- "And turn not your cheek in scorn towards people, nor walk in insolence through the earth, for God loves not the arrogant boaster." (31:18)
- "The proud will not enter Paradise, nor a violent speaker." (Hadith)
- "Be moderate in your pace, lower your voice for the harshest of sounds without doubt is the braying of the ass." (31:19)

Another important virtue mentioned in the Qur'an very frequently is *sabr*, or patience. "Be steadfast in patience" (11:115) is God's advice to counteract life's ups and downs. *Sabr* helps a person remain cool and rational when under stress, to be less angry and worried, and more tolerant and understanding. There are numerous verses in the Qur'an that advise people to strive for patience, such as:

- "Seek (God's) assistance through patience and *solat* for God is with the patient." (2:153)
- "Be firm and patient in pain and suffering, and adversity and throughout all periods of panic." (2:177)
- "And bear with patient constancy whatever befalls you for that is firmness of purpose in the conduct of affairs." (31:17)

These are comprehensive advices, covering any situation where patience is gravely required.

God even informs the believer that all prophets, including Prophet Abraham, Prophet Moses, Jesus Christ and Prophet Muhammad, were extremely patient in their respective arduous missions in the face of all sorts of persecution and hardships. God advises people: "Patiently persevere as did all prophets." (46:35)

Yet another important virtue in Islam is justice, which Islam commands people at all levels to observe, from the individuals, family members, society, the workplaces, organisations to the government. A few of the numerous Qur'anic verses on justice are:

- "O you who believe! Stand out firmly for justice." (4:135)
- "God orders that ... if you judge between people, you should judge justly." (4:58)
- "Do not let hatred of any people dissuade you from dealing justly. Be just: that is next to piety." (5:9)
- "God loves those who are fair and just." (49:9)

Virtues enhance the individual's attitude, conduct and character so that his whole self would "grow in purity".

CHARITY

Islam highly encourages the giving of charity to "those in need" (2:273).

Zakat (obligatory alms) is so important for the society that it forms the fourth of the Five Pillars of Islam.

The solat, the second Pillar of Islam, and zakat are always mentioned together in the Qur'an to stress the importance and closeness of these two righteous deeds, thus indicating that prayer without charity makes one's belief incomplete.

The command "Be steadfast in solat and practise regular zakat" (2:177) is repeated many times in the Qur'an in various ways. God says: "Establish regular solat and give regular zakat ... so that you will be blessed." (24:56) and that "Those who believe, and do deeds of righteousness, and establish solat and practise regular zakat, will have their reward with their Lord." (2:277)

Zakat literally means purification and growth. Thus, paying zakat purifies one's wealth and one's character from selfishness and greed.

It cultivates care and concern for the less fortunate, and instils gratitude for one's well-being.

There are two types of *zakat*: *zakatul mal* (*zakat* on wealth) and *zakat-fitrah* (*zakat* on one's self), both being annual contributions. As both alms are obligatory, the amount to be dispensed with is bound by certain conditions and rules.

In Singapore, Muslims give these alms to a Muslim institution like the Islamic Religious Council of Singapore (Muis) or to other Islamic bodies. These Islamic organisations would then disburse the money received to various categories of recipients and entitlements as stated in the Qur'an (9:60 & 2:273).

The *sadaqah* (charity), on the other hand, is a voluntary charitable act and is highly encouraged. Examples of this type of charity are donations to special development funds, to any charitable or welfare organisations, and to victims of disasters and any needy individuals.

In Islam, charity has value only if (1) something good and valuable is given, and (2) that which is given has to be honourably earned or acquired by the giver.

God informs Prophet Muhammad what to say when his people asked him what to give as charity: "(When) they ask you (O Muhammad!) what they should spend (in charity), say: 'Spend whatever that is good.'" (2:215) God also directly informs the believers: "O you who believe! Give of the good things which you have (honourably) earned." (2:267)

Abdullah Yusuf Ali, commenting on the above statement (2:215) in his translation of the Qur'an, *The Meaning of the Glorious Qur'an*, explains what constitutes charity, who should receive it, and how it should be given by answering three pertinent questions:

1. What shall we give?
   "Give anything that is good, useful, helpful and valuable. It may be property or money; it may be discarded clothes; it may be a helping hand; it may be advice; it may be a kind word: 'whatever that is good' is charity. But if the thing given is useless or harmful to the recipient, then the gift is worse than useless; it is positively harmful and the giver is a wrong-doer, and if you give a sword to a madman or drugs or even money to someone you want to corrupt, it is no charity but a gift of damnation."

2. To whom shall we give?

"It may be tempting to earn the world's praise by a gift that will be talked about, but are you meeting the needs of those who have the first claim on you? If you are not, it is no charity. Every gift is judged by its unselfish character."

3. How shall we give?

"In the sight of God, there should be no pretence, show and insincerity."

Spending on charity is praiseworthy, one that brings spiritual benefit. God says: "Spend in charity for the benefit of your own souls." (64:16)

GREETING OF PEACE

When two Muslims meet, whoever is faster says "*Assalamu-alaikum*" (Peace be on you) and the other replies, "*Wa-alaikum Salam*" (And peace be on you too). But most often, the reply would be longer: "*Wa Alaikum Salam Wa Rahmatullah*" (And to you be the Peace and Blessing of God.)

The above Islamic greeting is in direct response to God's command — that whoever offers his greeting first, the other is to return it in even better terms or at least in an equally courteous way. God says: "When a (courteous) greeting is offered to you, meet it with a greeting still more courteous, or (at least) of equal courtesy." (4:86)

The greeting of *salam* is offered at any time of the day or night when a Muslim meets another Muslim. The uniqueness of the Islamic greeting is embodied in the word "*salam*", which means "peace". The word is a symbolism for the indescribable Divine Bliss associated with God and Paradise. A few examples are:

- *Salam* (Peace) is one of the attributes of God: "God is ... the Source of Peace ..." (59:23)
- It is a word from God Himself: "Peace! (is) a Word (of salutation) from the Lord, Most Merciful." (36:58)
- It is used by God on His beloved prophets: "*Salam* on the prophets ..." (37:181) God even offered *salam* when He addressed them by name such as "*Salam* on Noah ..." (37:79), "*Salam* on Abraham ..." (37:109) and "*Salam* on Moses and Aaron ..." (37:120)

- Paradise is described as *Darus Salam* (Home of Peace) for the believers: "For them will be the Home of Peace ..." (6:127)
- The word is used among the dwellers of Paradise: "Their greeting therein will be 'Peace'." (14:23)

Muslims are taught to always initiate the *salam* at all times because of its intrinsic value. The Prophet said: "That person is closest to God who initiates *salam*."

When a Malay-Muslim meets another, and upon giving the verbal *salam*, he extends his right hand, clasps the person's extended hand for a moment and then each brings his hand to the chest over his heart. Women too do the same among themselves. This form of greeting — with words and action — enhances and promotes brotherhood, cordiality, closeness and goodwill, as well as humility and courtesy among Muslims. Muslims in some other parts of the world even hug after the verbal greeting is given.

Islam teaches Muslims to offer the *salam* even to Muslims they do not know, so as to cultivate the spirit of brotherhood in them. The Prophet said: "Your belief cannot be complete unless you love each other. Let me tell you something, which if you do, you will cultivate love between yourselves. Greet each other with *salam* whether the other person is known to you or not."

Letters and emails from Muslims to Muslims carry the salutation, "*Assalamu-alaikum Warahmatullahi Wabarakatu*" (May the Peace and Blessings of God be on you). On the phone, a Muslim starts his conversation with the *salam* and ends the conversation with it.

Muslims also apply the Prophet's teaching on greeting on the Prophet himself. Even though he has passed away, he is always near and dear to every Muslim. When mentioning the Prophet's name, they greet him with the salutation "*Sallallah alaihi wassallam*" in Arabic, which means "Peace be upon him". They also offer the *salam* to all other prophets like Jesus Christ and Prophet Moses when they mention their names during religious discourses.

The mode of greeting in Islam is a practical demonstration of the Islamic concept of peace, as the word "*salam*" is from the same root as "Islam", the Religion of Peace and Harmony.

11 ⛫WHOLESOME LIFESTYLE

To live in Islam is not merely to prepare for the Hereafter, but also to live a complete way of life right here in this material world. The Islamic advice is: eat, drink (non-alcoholic beverages) and be Muslim. "Muslim", in its root sense, is one who follows a lifestyle as advocated by Islam — totally submitting to God, totally pure and clean, totally wholesome.

As Islam does not separate the religious from the worldly, all Islamic practices have both spiritual and worldly values. To be pure and clean in all matters is so important in Islam that Prophet Muhammad declared: "Purity and cleanliness is half the Islamic faith."

PURITY AND CLEANLINESS

Purity and cleanliness are part of Islamic devotion. The faith aims at a total package of human development and enhancement not only in matters that concerns food or healthy living, but in all human dealings and communication. The whole package has to be *halal* (permissible under Islamic law).

Islam teaches Muslims to maintain purity and cleanliness by keeping away from anything and everything that jeopardises, or is disruptive to, his health as well as his physical, social and spiritual well-being.

The principle of cleanliness is even applied after one has relieved himself. Not only should the toilet be kept clean but also oneself after using it. A Muslim is required to clean himself using clean water after urination and defecation. This indeed has obvious hygiene benefits. Such "outward" or physical cleanliness is concerned with the body, clothes and the environment, but the terms "purity" and "cleanliness" extend beyond physical accomplishments. They include "inward" or non-physical concerns such as building one's character, personality and attitude positively, and keeping away from negative acts like corruption, fraud, malpractices and violence.

To be pure and clean at all times in both the physical (outward) and non-physical (inward) sense is part of the Islamic *Deen* (the believers' way of life). The Qur'an says that "God loves those who keep themselves pure and clean" (2:222).

HALAL PRINCIPLES

The principles of *halal* (allowed or lawful) and *haram* (prohibited or unlawful) are applied in a Muslim's daily activities, including food consumption, for the good of the individual, society, nation and humanity.

When a man does something praiseworthy — even a small act like helping a kitten that has fallen into a drain or picking up a broken glass from a playing field and throwing it in the rubbish bin — what he has done is *halal* and he gets spiritual merit for it. In contrast, if he indulges in or consumes anything that is destructive — in the physical or spiritual sense — to himself, people and the environment, his action is *haram*. For that, he sins or negates the goodness of his soul.

The following examples further illustrate the principles of *halal* and *haram*. Pork is *haram* but the meat of chicken is *halal*. However, the consumption of the *halal* chicken becomes *haram* if the person consuming it knows that:

- the (live) chicken was not slaughtered according to Islamic rites.
- the chicken was cooked with *haram* ingredients such as lard and alcohol.
- the chicken had been acquired in a *haram* way, for example, if it was stolen or bought with money earned from gambling which is a *haram* activity.

If he was tricked into consuming the chicken, or was absolutely unaware as to how it was obtained, he is not to be blamed and the burden of the sin falls on the guilty party.

Thus, the principles of *halal* and *haram* apply not only to food items but the whole range of activities a person does in his life. In other words, *halal* acts constitute *ibadah* (worship of God).

Prostitution, pimping and selling drugs, liquor or pornographic materials are all *haram* because these activities harm society. Earnings acquired through *haram* ways are *haram* too. There is also no excuse for indulging in *haram* activities even if the intentions are good, for example, a woman working as a prostitute to care for her children. Theft, aggression, terrorism and suicide bombings are all clear-cut *haram* actions.

In general, *haram* is declared on something because of the harm it causes to oneself, other people and the environment. Anything specifically mentioned in the Qur'an as *haram* is clear-cut prohibition, because it may be for spiritual matters beyond human understanding or findings. But some aspects depend on human research. For instance, a substance or activity that is considered harmless today due to lack of knowledge may be discovered to be harmful tomorrow from research findings. Newspapers often report such cases.

Not every action or thing falls under the *halal* and *haram* categories. There are others like *mubaah* and *makruh*. *Makruh*, for instance, is the act of doing something that is not *haram* but discouraged or undesirable.

Islam, as a way of life, provides guidance on *halal* and *haram* as a means for its followers to attain purity of the body and soul. God says that "the reward for those who keep themselves pure" is the "Gardens of Eternity" (20:76) — Paradise.

PROHIBITION OF CERTAIN ITEMS FOR CONSUMPTION

Muslims take *halal* food in obedience to God's command. To do otherwise is an act of impiety and is therefore a sin. Instructing people to be mindful of what they eat, God says:

- "O mankind! Eat of that which is *halal* (lawful) and good and follow not the ways of the devil." (2:168)
- "O you who believe! Eat of the good things that We (God) have provided for you." (2:172)
- "Lawful to you are all things good and pure ..." (5:5)

Pork is *haram* for Muslim consumption. God says: "(O you who believe!) Forbidden to you (for food) are ... the flesh of swine ..." (5:4) Still, pork is not the only item prohibited for consumption. The blood of *halal* animals and the meat of *halal* animals (like sheep) already dead before their slaughter is also prohibited. Even *halal* meat, if it fails to satisfy certain conditions, becomes *haram* for the consumption of believers. An example of these prohibitions is given in Chapter 5, verse 4 (numbered below for easy reference). God says: "(O you who believe!) Forbidden to you (for food) are:

1. dead meat
2. blood
3. the flesh of swine
4. that on which has been invoked the name of other than God
5. that which has been killed by strangling
6. or by a violent blow
7. or by a headlong fall
8. or by being gored to death
9. that which has been partly eaten by a wild animal, unless you can slaughter it before it dies
10. that which is sacrificed on stone (altars)
11. (forbidden) also is the division (of meat) by raffling with arrows (gambling): that is impiety."

The principles of *halal* and *haram* thus focus on the development and purification of the body and soul.

PROHIBITION OF ALCOHOL AND GAMBLING

Intoxicants and gambling are *haram* for Muslims. God says: "O you who believe! Intoxicants and gambling are an abomination of Satan's handiwork: Avoid such abomination that you may prosper. Satan's plan is to excite enmity and hatred among you with intoxicants and gambling, and hinder you from the remembrance of God and from the *solat*. Will you not then give up?" (5:93–94)

"Intoxicants" as mentioned in the Qur'an refers to any agent that causes the mind to befog and lose the ability to reason. Thus, intoxicants include alcohol, drugs, marijuana and cannabis. They are all *haram* in Islam, and indulging in them is sinful.

Before Islam, the social lifestyle of the people of Arabia centred on drinking and gambling. They were heavy drinkers and compulsive gamblers. With Islam, drinking and gambling became *haram* for their own good.

The prohibition of intoxicants and gambling is mentioned in the same verse because both are closely associated; both share similar characteristics and consequences. Gambling is also addictive and gives rise to problems similar to those of intoxicants. The Qur'an uses the phrase "abomination of Satan's handiwork" to refer to their possible dire consequences such as divorces, broken homes, fights and loss of dignity. Intoxicants and gambling can affect not only the abuser himself, but also his family members, social relationships and the society at large. Many marriages have broken down; many mature, even educated, people have ruined their lives; many parents have been shamed because of their children's indulgence in alcohol, drugs and gambling. Many of the air rages and outraging of modesty cases on aeroplanes and elsewhere (as frequently reported in the media) point to alcohol as being the main cause.

Experts have commented on the ills of alcohol. Dr Tan Chue Tin, consultant psychiatrist at Mount Elizabeth Hospital, Singapore, has this to say: "Alcohol does two things to a person. It dissolves moral constraints and social inhibitions. Second, it diminishes judgement." (*The New Paper*, 9 April 2006)

Social drinking is also *haram*, even taking small amounts of alcoholic beverages. This is because one can be easily influenced to drink more at social gatherings. It is also easy to turn to alcohol to drown one's worries. All problem drinkers and alcoholics indeed started out innocently as social drinkers. As a warning to this, the Prophet said: "What intoxicates when taken in big quantity is also *haram* to consume in small amounts."

HALAL FOOD

Islam commands believers to eat *halal* and wholesome food and drinks. God says: "O mankind! Eat of that which is *halal* and good and follow not the ways of the devil." (2:168) This verse provides three sets of advice. The first and second sets point to the fact that the food should be "lawful (*halal*) and "good" (*taiyib*), and the third states that when eating, a person must not "follow the ways of the devil".

Taiyib, which means clean and pure, refers to food that is wholesome and nourishing. "Follow not the ways of the devil" is concerned with cleanliness and moral etiquette. According to Muslim scholars, the statement refers to untidy places and dirty hands, overeating, gluttony and wasting food, for instance, piling one's plate with food at a buffet and leaving it half-eaten while blind to the fact that many people do not even get one proper meal a day.

Even in consuming *halal* food, Muslims are urged not to overeat. The Prophet said: "Muslims should be people who eat only when they are hungry." In encouraging moderate eating, the Prophet advised: "Kill not your heart with excessive eating" and "It is good to be always a little hungry."

The advice on *halal* food itself consists of two main features:

- the *halal* animal, like chicken, sheep and cattle, has to be slaughtered in the Islamic way as prescribed by God to make the meat *halal*.
- the food should be acquired through *halal* means.

In the first feature, slaughtering "in the Islamic way" refers to two sub-features: avoiding cruelty to the animal being slaughtered and draining away its blood.

The *halal* animal must be killed with as little pain as possible to make the meat *halal*. There should not be any cruelty inflicted on the animal being killed. When slaughtering a chicken, for instance, the Muslim uses a very sharp knife and runs it deeply in a circular motion under its neck without severing it. The deep cut in this location knocks out the animal within a couple of seconds.

It is a *haram* act to kill the chicken by twisting its neck, chopping off its neck, beating it to death or by plunging it into boiling water as these actions arrest the flow of blood from the animal's body. Blood is *haram* for consumption. It has to be drained away as naturally and as much as possible.

The second feature of *halal* food is concerned with personal values. The food should be bought with *halal* earnings, and not with money acquired through gambling, corruption, stealing, robbing, selling drugs, alcohol or prohibited items, which are all *haram* in Islam.

In Islam, eating is part of the total Islamic package of positive and gratifying living. It therefore teaches Muslims to eat only *halal* food, because such food impresses on the spiritual uplifting, well-being and health of the individual believer.

12 ISLAMIC DRESS CODE

Islam advocates a decent society. It therefore provides guidance to men and women in the way they should dress to guard their modesty in public. One of these ways is to cover their *aurah* (parts of the body that should not be exposed).

The *aurah* of a woman is her whole body except the face and hands. The *aurah* of a man extends from the navel to the knees.

The Qur'anic advice on modesty is meant for the spiritual good of both the males and females and as a way to promote positive moral values in the society. Being a global religion, Islam does not insist that Muslims throughout the world must wear Arabic dress. The attire of any race or culture can be worn as long as it fulfils the requirement of the Islamic dress code.

WOMEN'S MODESTY

God says that a believing woman should "guard her modesty and not display her beauty" (24:31). In the gentle and elegant expression of the Qur'an, this basically means that she should not "expose her body". Thus, a Muslim woman who covers certain parts of her body is merely heeding the commands of God on this aspect to attain and enhance her spiritual purity and earn the love of God.

In "guarding her modesty", she keeps away from transparent clothes, body-hugging dresses, short skirts, high-slit skirts and sleeveless and low-cut blouses. Instead she wears long-sleeved blouses, long skirts or pants, *sarungs* (sheath-like attire, covering the lower part of the body from waist to ankle), the *baju kurung* (Malay costume comprising a long blouse and *sarung*) or any outfit that covers her decently. She covers her head with a scarf or wears the *jilbab* (the headdress that covers the head down to the shoulders) but leaves her face and hands uncovered.

A Muslim woman who covers up Islamically earns spiritual merits. She is taught that the earlier in her life she starts wearing Islamically-approved attire, the better it is for her well-being both in the worldly and spiritual sense. Often, she begins observing the Islamic dress code upon reaching puberty as advised by Prophet Muhammad who said: "A girl who has attained puberty should start covering her whole body except her face and hands." Others would begin to wear the headscarf at some time in their matured lives or from the time they perform the Haj or Umrah.

A Singaporean public figure, who holds a law degree, said about her Islamic attire (as reported in *The Straits Times*): "I dress the way I do for religious reasons. People will accept you for what you are, what you stand for and the contributions you make."

A Muslim female student said: "The Islamic dress code provides the Muslim woman the right to keep her body sacred and not made to be exploited and gawked at by men. Thus, Islam's advice to women to observe modesty is actually to provide status and respect to them."

Yet another Muslim woman, who has been wearing the Malay dress and covering her head with a *tudung* (headscarf) since her undergraduate days, said: "In Islam, every woman is given the opportunity to attain the highest level of piety at all times. There is no restriction as to the colour, fashion or cultural origin of the dress. As a Muslim woman can be of any race — Indian, Malay, Chinese, American or English — she can observe the Islamic dress code in any fashion she desires. In my case, although I am a Malay, apart from the Malay dress, I have worn Iranian dress, Punjabi dress, and even Vietnamese dress and pant suit. Does not that make me a global person? Still the dress is Islamic.

"The dress code of Islam is actually a liberating force for women. Definitely, wearing Islamic dress, which includes the headdress, does not deter our thinking ability or our intellectual capability. The Muslim woman observes the Islamic dress code to obey God and to uplift and maintain her spiritual purity."

Why a greater restriction is imposed on women in the way they dress is obvious. One man said: "It is easier for a woman to arouse the sexual feeling of a man by just uncovering some parts of her body than the other way round. Scantily- or sexily-dressed women (even in movies, pictures in the mass media and on the Internet) could be the initiator of sexual crimes in one form or another. Almost every day, newspapers report sexual crimes committed by males as young as in their early teens and as old as in their late sixties. Often, innocent girls who dress decently unfortunately become victims of criminals with 'stored up' emotions, men who had been indulging their sight at every 'sexual' opportunity they get or of images in public or private. May I ask: who would be ogled at by a man, a woman who wears a tight or revealing outfit, or one who is decently dressed?"

The Muslim woman who truly understands the implication of the command of God regarding modesty observes the Islamic dress code to safeguard her modesty as well as promote decency in the society. But most importantly, she is adhering to Islamic teachings on modesty by wearing the *hijab* (Islamic attire) as best as she can. A Muslim woman once remarked: "Mary, the mother of Jesus Christ, is described in the Qur'an honourably as a 'woman of all nations'. And she is always seen in Christian paintings wearing the *hijab*."

TOTAL SECLUSION
Muslim women in some countries wear an enveloping outer garment over their clothes that covers the whole of their bodies, often including their faces. This type of garment is commonly referred to as the *purdah* or *burqa*, suggesting total seclusion.

Though Muslim scholars are divided over this issue of female modesty, some saying women should be totally covered, many other scholars nowadays say that the Qur'anic verses on this subject depend on interpretations and that the use of these head-to-toe robes:

- is not an instruction from the Qur'an.
- was not introduced by Islam.
- was already in existence in some countries even before the advent of Islam.

What is commonly worn by the majority of Muslim women in Indonesia, Malaysia, Singapore and other parts of Asia — and even by many in the Middle-East countries — is what they refer to as *hijab*, a word that describes Islamic modesty or the act of covering up the whole body in any cultural or general attire, leaving only the face and hands below the wrists exposed. To cover the head and hair, they use headscarves, often in various styles, called *tudung* in Malay.

The Prophet had said that female modesty means that the whole body should be covered except the face and hands. Even when a female pilgrim is in *ihram* (state of complete devotion) for the Haj or Umrah, it is strictly forbidden for her to carry out her pilgrimage rituals with her face covered. She has to leave her face and hands (below the wrists) uncovered.

Muslim women heed God's advice on modesty in different ways, often according to their individual understanding or the tradition of the society they live in.

MEN'S MODESTY

In Islam, men too have to "guard their modesty" in order to attain "greater purity".

Muslim men are discouraged from wearing above-the-knee shorts as the *aurah* for men extends from the navel to the knees. In addition, men are advised to "lower their gaze" at women.

From the Islamic perspective, when a woman flaunts her body, she sins. The man, who ogles at the woman, even if she is a non-Muslim, equally sins as men are also commanded, in the Qur'an, to avert their gaze. God says: "The believing men should lower their gaze and guard their modesty so as to attain greater purity." (24:30)

The committing of sex crimes depends on the conscience and spiritual standing of the man, the "weaker" he is, the easier he succumbs to sexual attraction and promiscuity.

While the dress code for a Muslim woman includes the covering of the head, there is no requirement for a Muslim man to cover his head. However, it is a *Sunnah* (practice of Prophet Muhammad) to do so. Some Muslim men, therefore, begin to wear a Haji cap from the time they return from the Haj. Many men cover their heads during religious functions and when performing the *solat* in the home or mosque as an act of devotion and humility.

13 🕌 MARRIAGE AND DIVORCE

Marriage is a religious sacrament. Plural marriages, commonly known as polygamy, are permitted for various people in some Muslim societies. However, Islam did not introduce the practice. It only regulated its practice to give rights and status to women. Plural marriages in the Middle-East predate Islam by many centuries. The rich practised polygamy with unlimited number of wives. Women had no rights, status or earnings, and were treated as mere chattels.

Islam limited the number of wives a man could have, and introduced a systematic marriage regulation with rules on how to be a responsible husband. The Islamic norm is monogamy: "(marry) only one" (4:3).

Divorce is permitted only as a last resort, when a husband and his wife come to a point of irreparable crisis in their marriage.

MARRIAGE

Nikah (marriage), though a civil contract, is a sacred bond between a man and a woman. God says that a man should seek marriage "desiring chastity, not lust" (4:24).

The most important requirement of a Muslim marriage is the *ijab kabul* (marriage solemnisation). The dower (dowry) or wedding gift, also important, is given by the prospective husband to his bride. It can be in the form of money, property or jewellery, depending on what the groom can afford. God says: "(Upon marriage), give the women their dower as a gift." (4:4) The other requirements of an Islamic marriage are:

- that the woman must consent to the marriage.
- that the man should not take back the dower given to her even in the event of a divorce between them.

- the husband should be loving towards his wife.

God says: "O you who believe! You are forbidden to marry women against their will. Nor should you treat them with harshness." (4:19) and that "Even if you had given them loads of treasure for dower, take not the least bit of it back." (4:20)

The *nikah* ceremony can be conducted at any place such as at the Registrar of Muslim Marriages, the mosque or at home.

The *kadi* (marriage official) solemnises the couple before representatives from the households of the couple. The ceremony begins with the *kadi* getting the marriage consent from the prospective bride and groom. Then, the groom, with his hand clasped in *salam* with that of the *kadi*, pronounces the marriage vow which includes his bride's name and the dower he is giving to her. The *kadi* proceeds by giving the *khutbah* (sermon) during which he advises the groom to take good care of his wife and vice versa, and spells out the responsibilities of both the husband and wife as a general address for all present to hear and apply it in their own married lives too. After the sermon, the *kadi* recites a *do'a* to conclude the ceremony.

A marriage is a happy occasion because two unrelated families are being united and enlarged. As Islam recognises no barriers in ethnicity, inter-racial marriages are not frowned upon.

POLYGAMY

Islam teaches Muslims to seek marriage desiring "chastity, not lewdness, not secret intrigues" (5:6). There should be no mistresses or secret relationships.

God says: "… marry women of your choice, two or three or four. But if you fear you shall not be able to deal justly (with them), then (marry) only one …" (4:3) Here, God asserts that a man may have up to four wives on condition that he is able to "deal justly" with everyone of them, otherwise he should take only one wife.

According to Muslim scholars, the phrase "deal justly" means that: (1) his second marriage, for instance, should not result in the divorce of his first wife if the marriage has been happy all along, and (2) the husband has to show equality to all his wives in all aspects of honourable living, including love, companionship, protection and maintenance.

In other words, if a man has more than one wife, he should treat his wives equally, both materially and emotionally, and maintain and promote happiness and harmony in the family. Such an equal treatment, beyond the realm of wealth, is very difficult to carry out. Indeed God warns: "You will not be able to treat the wives with equality, however much you desire that." (4:129) In other words, whoever takes multiple wives and fails to fulfil the obligations required would be answerable to God in the Hereafter.

Thus, Islam permits limited polygamy, but with an emphasis on equal treatment for the wives. Islam puts "No" to alcohol, "No" to pork, but in matters of the heart and marriage, an emphatic "Marry one only and no divorce" is not imposed due to considerations of circumstances and human failings. Muslim marriages, including regulations on plural marriages, and divorces come under the purview of the Shari'ah (Islamic Law) of a Muslim country or a registered Muslim institution in a secular country.

DIVORCE

Divorce between a married couple is allowed in Islam when the conjugal harmony between them is destroyed to such an extent that it is no longer possible for both the husband and wife to live together in peace.

Divorce is a solution to an unsuccessful marriage. Without this facility, the incompatible married couple would have to live an intolerable and unhappy life. On the other hand, for a marriage that has gone terribly awry, a divorce provides the chance for each party to live a renewed life, even giving them the opportunity of marrying new partners.

Islam cautions against any hasty action in seeking a divorce as it involves many moral and social issues and affects family relationships. Divorce is therefore taken as a last resort when all efforts to help the couple (4:35), by friends and relatives of both husband and wife or a professional institution, to resolve the problem is unsuccessful.

The implementation of a divorce is safeguarded by two *talak* (divorce pronunciations) only. This means that the couple can remarry each other after the first and even the second *talak*. However, if they divorce for the third time, it is almost impossible for them to marry each other again. God says: "A divorce is only permissible twice: after that the parties should either hold together on equitable terms or separate with kindness." (2:229)

Thus, the mere pronouncing of the *talak* (namely, "I divorce you") three times by the husband, made one after another in a fit of anger or emotion, does not nullify a marriage bond. Islam encourages the parties to come to a term of forgiveness and live in peace. God says: "... it is no sin for the two of them if they make terms of peace between themselves. Peace is better." (4:128)

A divorce has to be carried out in a proper and respectful way before witnesses just as the marriage solemnisation was conducted seriously in the first place.

When an application for a divorce is filed, the Shari'ah Court of a country acts as an arbiter (4:34), aimed at seeking a harmonious reconciliation between the two parties.

The court allows only the first and second *talak* to take place, each after a lapse of time to give the affected parties time to think over or to allow a "cooling down" period for possible reconciliation. God advises husbands initiating a divorce thus: "Either take them back on equitable terms or set them free on equitable terms, do not take them back to injure them, or to take unfair advantage ..." (2:231)

The third *talak* is often undertaken much later when all reconciliatory efforts and professional counselling fail.

In a divorce, the man would have to maintain his former wife. God says: "For divorced women, maintenance (should be provided) on a reasonable (scale). This is a duty on the righteous." (2:242) Details of the maintenance procedures and other advice are given in Chapter 2 of the Qur'an, from verses 228 to 239.

Because of the heavy burden on man when a divorce takes place, he is given some advantage in repudiating the marriage so he would think twice before initiating the *talak*. But, Islam also gives women the right to seek a divorce. God says: "Women shall have rights similar to the rights against them." (2:228) A woman may seek divorce for a number of reasons such as failure to provide maintenance, desertion and cruelty on the part of her husband.

Divorce is abhorred in Islam. Prophet Muhammad said: "Of all things permitted, the most displeasing to God is divorce."

14 🕌HUMAN AND ANIMAL RIGHTS

Human beings, as the most intelligent beings created, have been entrusted with the responsibility of caring not only for themselves but also for animals and the environment.

Islam gave status to women, a move unprecedented in the history of religions. It exalted their position at a time when women all over the world were treated inferior to men.

The giving of status to women was one of the reasons why the pagan Meccans were unhappy with Islam and fought to annihilate it. In their tradition, women held no rights and position. Women and girls could even be bought and sold at will. In Islam, women are held in honour and their rights recognised in such areas as in social life, education, marriage, property and inheritance.

RIGHTS OF WOMEN
Women have rights just like those of men. God says: "Women shall have rights similar to the rights against them." (2:228) In Chapter 4 of the Qur'an, called "An-Nisaa" which means "The Women", many of the verses in it deal with the rights of women and with matters relating to family life in general.

Women can work in honourable jobs, and may keep whatever they earn. God says: "To men is allotted what they earn and to women what they earn." (4:32) In other words, a man cannot take away his wife's earnings by force or as a rule. She may, on her free will, share her earnings with her husband to help out the family.

A Muslim woman also has absolute right to keep, sell or manage her property in her own way, including the property acquired by her as her marriage gift. Her husband cannot take it back even in a divorce.

God says: "Even if you had given her loads of treasure for dower, take not the least bit of it back." (4:20)

A woman's right to inheritance is also defined. God says: "... there is a share for women, a determined share, be the property large or small." (4:7) (The "share" is mentioned in detail in verse 11 of the same chapter.) Other passages in the Qur'an on women's position and status include:

- "Men are the protectors and maintainers of women because God has given the one more (strength) than the other." (4:34)
- "O you who believe! You are forbidden to ... treat (women) with harshness." (4:19)

Here are some teachings of Prophet Muhammad on the subject:

- "The rights of women are sacred. See therefore, that women are maintained in the rights granted to them."
- "A Muslim must not hate his wife; and if he be displeased with one bad disposition in her, then let him be pleased with another which is good."
- "The best of you are those who behave well to your wives and treat them well."
- "God commands you to treat women well, for they are your mothers, daughters and aunts."
- "Paradise lies at the feet of mothers."

Females have the same rights and opportunities as males to pursue education as high as their intellectual capability can take them. The Prophet said: "The acquisition of knowledge is the obligation of every Muslim, male or female."

Husbands and wives are given equal rights of protection, care and love. The splendid imagery used in the Qur'an on equal rights goes thus: "Your wives: they are your garment and you are their garment." (2:187) Husband and wife are each other's garment, fitting into each other as a garment fits the body. It provides mutual support, comfort and protection.

All these Qur'anic passages and the Prophet's words form the foundation for further progression of the Islamic-based rights of Muslim women today.

RIGHTS OF PARENTS

Parents hold an honourable position in Islam. This is reflected in the following statements made by Prophet Muhammad:

- "The secret of pleasing God lies in the pleasing of one's father, and the cause of annoying God lies in annoying one's father."
- "He who wishes to do good and enter Paradise must please his father and mother."

God instructs: "Do good to your parents ..." (4:36 & 6:151) This command, "Do good", is used in a very comprehensive sense and includes all the virtues that should be showered on parents such as love, respect, obedience, honour, consideration and due rights. God advises everyone whose parents are still living: "Treat your parents with kindness ..." (2:83)

Disrespect towards parents, offending and cursing them are considered acts of ingratitude and therefore sinful. The Prophet said: "A man's reviling of his parents is one of the serious sins."

The honour and respect due to parents are only second to the honour and respect due to God. The Qur'an says: "Your Lord has decreed that you worship none but Him, and that you be kind to parents. Whether one or both attain old age in your life-time, say not to them a word of contempt, nor repel them, but address them in terms of honour." (17:23–24) In these two verses, the following important instructions are given:

- Be kind and dutiful to your parents.
- Do not speak harshly to them.
- Do not treat them as useless beings in their old age.
- Honour them (but not to the extent of worshipping them).

These instructions are meant to develop in a person the willing desire to care for his parents, especially in their old age. God advises: "Bear them company in this life with justice and consideration and follow the way of those who turn to Me in love." (31:15)

In the exquisite language of the Qur'an, the phrase "bear them company" expresses a load of meaning. It shows that, when parents become old, their children should be close to them and take care of them in their own homes. They should give their elderly parents love, protection and support to see them through the rest of their lives.

God wants a person to show gratitude to his parents by making him aware of the pains and hardship his mother had to endure when he was in her womb, during his birth and in the first couple of his most difficult and delicate years of childhood. God says: "We have enjoined on man (to be good) to his parents. His mother bore him by bearing hardship, and his utter dependence on her lasted two years: (Hear the command, O man!): Show gratitude to Me and to your parents ..." (31:14)

In this verse, the word "man" is specifically used instead of "child" in order to draw attention to the fact that a child does not ignore his mother, but an adult usually does, especially upon getting married. God, therefore, commands a person to show gratitude, first, to God because he owes Him his whole existence, and second, to his parents because he owes them his early life. "Gratitude" here means paying back — by bearing "them company in this life with justice and consideration" (31:15).

The sincere display of these virtues towards parents would not go unrewarded. Children who take care of their parents in their old age would themselves be taken care of by their children later on. The Prophet said: "Be of good service to your parents for surely your children will be of good service to you."

Apart from the virtues to be accorded to one's parents, God also advises a Muslim to say a do'a for them regardless of whether they are still alive or have passed away. The do'a goes: "O My Lord! Bestow Your grace upon them as they had cherished and reared me when I was a child." (17:24)

RIGHTS OF NEIGHBOURS

Prophet Muhammad, in recognising the importance of neighbours in human relationship, said: "He is not a Muslim who eats his fill while his neighbour starves."

In Islam, a fellow student, a colleague at the workplace or a fellow traveller are all regarded as neighbours. God loves "Those who do good to those in need, neighbours who are near, neighbours who are strangers, the companion by your side, the wayfarer (you meet) (but) God loves not the arrogant, the vain-glorious, nor those who are niggardly ..." (4:36)

In this verse, Muslims are commanded not only to be good but also to do good to their neighbours. Examples of "doing good", as listed out in a saying of the Prophet, are:

- Help him if he asks your help.
- Give him relief if he seeks your relief.
- Lend him if he needs a loan.
- Show him concern if he is distressed.
- Congratulate him if he meets any good.
- Sympathise with him if any calamity befalls him.
- Do not block his air by raising your building high without his permission.
- Harass him not.
- Give him a share when you buy fruits, and if you do not give him, bring what you buy quietly and let not your children take them out to excite the jealousy of his children.
- Nurse him when he is ill.
- Attend his funeral when he dies.

The Muslim ought also to make his neighbours, as well as others in general, feel safe with him. The following sayings of the Prophet bear this out:

- "He is not truly a believer if his neighbour is not safe from his actions."
- "The believer is he who is not a danger to the life and property of other people."
- "A Muslim is he who avoids harming people with his tongue and hands."

Apart from their safety, the Muslim should be friendly and establish rapport and goodwill with them. He has to extend the spirit of neighbourliness by approaching his new neighbours first, bringing gifts like fruits or biscuits as a token of the friendship.

A Muslim's neighbours, be they Muslims or non-Muslims, must be treated alike with respect. He must not be "arrogant, vain-glorious or niggardly" to them (as commanded in 4:36). The Prophet said: "The best believer in God's sight is the one who behaves best to his neighbours."

RIGHTS OF ANIMALS

Many Islamic rules and regulations focus on creatures because, like plants and trees, they play an important role in the intricate and interdependent network of the ecosystems of the earth, and are also at the mercy of human failings.

Prophet Muhammad had, on numerous occasions, asked people to treat animals with kindness. Animals should not be burdened beyond what they can bear. They should also not be injured or tortured. They (domestic animals or those in the zoo) should be well fed and well looked after.

Muslims do not eat pork as a religious ruling, but they have to observe the rules on animal treatment: No Muslim should ill-treat or be cruel to pigs.

When Muslims slaughter a *halal* animal for food, they slaughter it in a kind and efficient manner so as to inflict the least pain and torture before it dies.

Some advice given by the Prophet on animal rights are:

- "Fear God concerning animals. Ride them when they are in a good condition and retire them in good health (without putting it to excessive work)."
- "Let the camel graze well wherever there is greens but travel fast if the land is parched and dry so that the animal would arrive quickly at its destination and be saved from thirst and hunger on the way."
- "If a person unjustly kills a bird (other than for food), he will have to answer for it before God. One is not allowed to kill any animal for the sake of sport or game." (Cockfight or bullfight is a cruel sport forbidden in Islam.)
- "Showing kindness to an animal — any animal — is an act which is rewarded by God." (He was praising a traveller who saw a thirsty dog, went to a well, filled his leather bag with water and offered it to the dog.)
- "Do it well when you slaughter an animal. And each one of you should sharpen his knife, give comfort to the animal, slaughter it in such a way that its life departs quickly without suffering." (Muslims slaughter animals for food in this way with a short prayer.)

Certain creatures, such as termites, rats, crows and bees, have their rights, too. So when they have to be exterminated for valid purposes, the process should be done without inflicting suffering to them.

Why must animals have rights? Why must they be treated well? God answers: "There is not an animal (that lives) on earth (including in the sea), nor a creature that flies on its wings but (forms part of) communities like you." (6:38)

Abdullah Yusuf Ali, in his commentary on this verse in *The Meaning of the Glorious Qur'an*, says: "In our pride we may exclude animals from our purview, but they all live a life, social and individual, like ourselves, and all life is subject to the Plan and Will of God."

In Islam, man has been given the responsibility of working in righteous ways to enhance harmony not only with fellow humans but also with all living creatures. This is God's *amanah* (trust) to man.

15 ⛰WORSHIP OF GOD

Islam is called the *Deen* (the believers' way of life) in the Qur'an. A Muslim, therefore, during his *solat*, makes a pledge thus: "Verily, my *solat* and my sacrifice, my life and my death are all for God, Lord of the Worlds." (6:162) This pledge contains the sum of all his actions on earth. Thus, all actions undertaken in accordance with God's command come under the all-encompassing term "*ibadah*" (worship of God).

As Islam has provided comprehensive guidance on how to observe *ibadah*, the onus in fulfilling it lies on the person. The Prophet said: "A man shall be asked three things on Judgement Day: concerning his life, how he lived it; concerning his wealth, how he acquired it and in what way he spent it; concerning his knowledge, what he did with it."

CONCEPT OF ISLAMIC WORSHIP

Ibadah comprises three main components: *iman* (faith), *amal solih* (righteous deeds or works), and all worldly engagements taken for livelihood in the name of God.

In Islam, faith alone is insufficient for entry into Paradise. Righteous deeds or works are components of a practical Islam together with what and how one seeks his livelihood.

To worship God means to submit or surrender to Him, and that means following His Instructions and Guidance. In other words, *ibadah* refers to any action undertaken for righteous living (faith and spiritual) and for the fulfilment of life on earth. So, carrying out the daily responsibilities and commitments is part of Islamic worship. That means pursuing education is *ibadah*, to work as an engineer or a clerk or a labourer is also *ibadah*. To observe the Islamic dress code, to cook the family meals, to eat *halal* food, to strive to build up conduct and character, to establish friendship and to help the poor and needy are all part and parcel of *ibadah*.

There are numerous verses in the Qur'an that provide guidance on *ibadah*. In Chapter 17, verses 23 to 37 alone, 12 commandments are given as guidance. They are given in detail in the Qur'an but here they are summarised as follows:

1. Worship none but God (17:23).
2. Be kind to your parents (17:23–24).
3. Help your relatives and the wayfarer (including the needy) (17:26).
4. Do not be spendthrift, or niggardly (that is, stingy) but keep a just balance between these two extremes (17:27–29).
5. Do not kill (or give away) your children for fear of want (17:31).
6. Do not commit adultery (17:32).
7. Do not kill (17:32).
8. Do not touch the property of orphans, unless it be to their (orphans') benefit (17:34).
9. Fulfil your undertakings and responsibilities (17:34).
10. Do not cheat but be fair in your business and other dealings (17:35).
11. Do not indulge in idle talk or about things you have no knowledge of (17:36).
12. Do not be proud or boastful (17:37).

The dos and don'ts mentioned in the above verses deal with a wide spectrum of human activities from religious to social to business dealings. Many other verses in the Qur'an deal with other aspects of human life.

Ibadah is the substance or complete package of Islamic living that promotes growth of discipline, culture, core values and society, and includes maintaining inter-religious and inter-racial harmony, and contribution to the peace, prosperity and progress of humanity.

SIGNIFICANCE OF JIHAD

One of the elements of daily responsibilities and commitments is striving for success in life. In the Islamic context, striving is called "jihad", a part of daily life.

Basically, jihad refers to the effort a Muslim must put in to preserve Islam, to attain spiritual purity and to improve oneself. Jihad therefore is a religious duty of every Muslim.

The first meaning of jihad applies to the striving to preserve Islam. Muslims preserve Islam by following the teachings of Islam closely and by being righteous.

In history, Muslims often had to defend Islam when their freedom to practise the religion was transgressed. Jihad was undertaken to promote justice and peace. Hence, jihad also refers to the striving of Muslims against all forms of injustice and oppression committed against them. Serious and knowledgeable Muslims would not use the word indiscriminately or use it to mean "holy war".

Jihad is not a Qur'anic term for holy war. In fact, in Islam, there is no such a thing as a holy war because of the fact that a war cannot be holy. A war is a sad and unfortunate outcome when all negotiations for peace fail. Muslims are forbidden to be the aggressor or to start a war. However, they are allowed to fight back in self-defense when attacked. Still, they must immediately stop fighting when peace is offered. God says: "When the enemy inclines towards peace, incline also to it." (8:61)

The second meaning of jihad applies to the striving to strictly observe Islamic practices of *solat*, fasting and other acts of Islamic righteousness, as well as striving to fight against spiritual decadence and striving to attain spiritual purity by dispelling wrongdoing and evil temptations, such as corruption and sexual promiscuity. God says: "And strive hard for God such a striving as is due to Him." (22:78). Here, jihad is the spiritual striving to attain closeness to God by observing Islamic practices and righteousness.

The third meaning of jihad applies to the striving to improve oneself through moral values and education to live a dignified life on earth.

Thus, jihad, according to the Qur'an, has great significance in the everyday life of the Muslim. He has to strive to preserve Islam, to attain spiritual purity and improve himself in education and character. None of these righteous undertakings can be achieved without striving (jihad).

REWARD FOR STRIVING

Striving to attain success is a praiseworthy act in Islam. As Islam does not separate the "worldly" from the "religious" or "spiritual", striving for success applies to both this world and the next. Thus, "worldly" work and "religious" work are combined and are part and parcel of *ibadah*.

Prophet Muhammad said: "The most meritorious concern is that of the true believer who struggles for success in this earthly life and for the Hereafter."

Islam lays down the principle of striving for success in the most unequivocal terms, pointing out that any one who does not strive should not expect to be successful. God says: "Man shall have nothing but what he strives for." (53:39)

Islam makes it known that if a person wants to reap success in any endeavour, he must put effort to achieve it. God says: "For each is that which he has earned and against each is only that which he has deserved." (2:286) Thus, when a person strives, he gets what he strove for.

Reward is guaranteed to those who strive; the more efficient and productive his effort, the better the reward. God says: "That (the fruit of) his striving will soon come to sight; then will he be rewarded with a reward complete." (53:40–41)

PRAISE FOR WORKING

All honest and legitimate work, for example the student's schoolwork, the housewife's household chores and the wage-earner's responsibilities, is Islamic and forms the lifeblood of human progress. God says: "Work, and God will see your work." (9:105) God judges a person's work according to what he has done and how he has done it.

Prophet Muhammad himself led by example. No work was too low for him. He cleaned his house, assisted his wife in the household chores, and laboured in many kinds of work with his companions and followers. He never despised any work, thus demonstrating through his personal examples that every kind of work dignifies man.

Workers are described by the Prophet as being near to God in such terms as: "One who earns his livelihood (by the sweat of his brow) is God's beloved." and "The worker is a friend of God."

God showers His blessings on people who work hard in a craft, profession or business for their sustenance and general progress. The following maxims from the Prophet bear this out:

- "God likes to see the believer working at his job."
- "Indeed God likes the one who has a craft (skill)."
- "The one who earns his sustenance in *halal* ways through his efforts is a beloved of God."

Islam gives a Muslim full liberty to choose any work according to his individual capacity and taste, but the work must satisfy the Islamic conditions of righteousness. The righteous way of seeking a livelihood is a service to the family and the community, and therefore to God. Honesty in work is so important that the Prophet said: "Next to the *solat* is the obligation of earning an honest living." He also said: "The honest merchant (businessman) is with the prophets and the truthful ones."

Islam forbids workers to encroach on the possessions of others or adopt deceitful and illegal ways of earning their livelihood. An employee has to distance himself from bribery and all forms of corruption. God says: "And swallow not your wealth among yourselves by false means, nor seek to gain access to other people's property (through corruption) …" (2:188)

Islam also abhors idleness, laziness and begging. Confining or retiring to a corner as an ascetic, making no effort to improve one's living conditions and doing no work to earn a living are all un-Islamic.

The Prophet's advice on avoiding being a burden to society includes:

- "Beg not anything from people."
- "The best person is one who is most useful to his people."
- "Whoever is able and fit and does not work for himself or for others, God is not gracious to him."
- "No one eats better food than that which he eats out of the work of his own hand."
- "He who seeks the world lawfully, refrains from begging, caters for his family, and is kind to his neighbours, will meet God with his face shining like the full moon."

Islam also urges Muslims to be wary of the choices of work as it prohibits the earning of one's living by *haram* means, such as prostitution and gambling. Selling drugs and alcoholic beverages are also *haram* as this can harm people who consume them. Smuggling, robbery, theft, shoplifting, bribery (those who offer as well as those who receive), breach of trust and corruption, such as embezzlement of public or corporate money, are all prohibited.

Islam urges every individual to work efficiently and conscientiously, and attain a high level of productivity. The following sayings of the Prophet focus on such values:

- "A worker who excels in his devotion to God and also renders to his employer the duty, sincerity and obedience that he owes him, for him there is double reward (with God)."
- "God desires that when you perform a job, you must do it perfectly."

Advising people that a job should be carried out conscientiously, the Prophet said: "Work for the next world as if you were going to die tomorrow, and work for this world as if you would never die."

MEANING OF RIGHTEOUSNESS

Righteousness is doing good deeds or good works. God says: "Whoever does good works and has faith, his endeavour will not be rejected." (21:94)

In Islam, *iman* (belief) and *amal solih* (righteous deeds or works) are to be put into practice in tandem. They are so closely linked that they are often generally mentioned together in the Qur'an and the Hadith. The Qur'an says: "... righteous is he who believes in God, and the Last Day and the Angels and the Scripture and the Prophets, and gives his wealth, for the love of Him, to kinsfolk and to orphans and the needy and the wayfarer and to those who ask, and to set slaves free, and observes the *solat* and pays the *zakat* (obligatory alms)." (2:177)

Guidance on good deeds is also given by Prophet Muhammad:

- "Certainly God does not look at your appearance or your wealth; He looks at your heart and your deeds."
- "Assist any oppressed person whether Muslim or non-Muslim."
- "For him who helps one who is in distress, God will record 73 acts of pardon."

- "He is not a believer who eats his fill while his neighbour (Muslim or non-Muslim) is hungry."

God promises bliss to those who do good deeds. He says:

- "God loves those who do good." (4:96)
- "As to the righteous, they will be in the midst of Gardens ..." (51:15) In Qur'anic allegory, "Gardens" stands for "Paradise". It symbolises the highest level of satisfaction and bliss.
- "Whoever works righteousness, man or woman, and has faith, verily to him will We give a new life, a life that is good and pure, and We will bestow on such their reward according to the best of their actions." (16:97)

The opportunity to do good works or righteousness is right now, when one is living. The Prophet said: "When a man dies, his righteous works stop, except three: his acts of charity which are continued by his family members; his knowledge by which the living may benefit, and his pious issue (offspring) who prays for him."

16 🕌 GLOBAL EDUCATION

Islam commands Muslims to acquire education from anywhere in the world and to be progressive. It encourages them to exercise their mind and use their reasoning in all matters, worldly as well as spiritual. Reason is so important to human beings that Prophet Muhammad said: "Reason is the root of my faith (Islam)."

The Qur'an, though basically a religious Book, does touch on certain principles and laws governing life and the universe, implying that Islam is not against science and global education. Instead, it encourages the learning of any branch of the sciences, including the proper use of the "bounties" God has given us on earth and in the universe.

FORMAL LEARNING

"Read!" This is the very first word in Islam, an important word of action in education and training. The word appears as a command in the very first Revelation Prophet Muhammad received from God: "Read! In the name of your Lord ..." (96:1) Islam greatly values knowledge and learning.

There are two categories of knowledge — religious and worldly — each complementing the other. The religious knowledge that a Muslim learns is concerned with *fardhu 'ain* (personal obligation) like the *solat* and the Ramadan fast. *Fardhu 'ain* supports the structure of a Muslim's life and makes him aware of the Hereafter as well as the need to live righteously on this earth.

Fardhu kifayah (communal obligation) includes worldly sciences. It helps to develop the mind, the intellect and the social environment, and aims to ensure that the Muslim is equipped adequately with all the things necessary to enable him to live comfortably and productively.

Fardhu 'ain and *fardhu kifayah* are not separated as both are meant for the good of the individual, the community, the country and the world in general. The Muslim is therefore advised to strike a balance between his spiritual needs and his material requirements. The Prophet said: "The most correct concern of a true believer is to pay attention to matters of this world and to the matters pertaining to the Hereafter."

Encouraging people to learn and acquire knowledge was always on the lips of the Prophet. He also said: "Go even to China to pursue knowledge." This advice comprises three features: China was considered a faraway land from Arabia in those days; it was culturally more advanced than many other countries, and it was totally non-Muslim as Islam had not yet spread to China. Thus, the advice conveys the message that Muslims ought to obtain knowledge and training even if the place of learning is far away from his country and even if the required knowledge is available from non-Muslims. All useful knowledge has no restriction or nationality as it comes from one source — God.

Some quotations from the Hadith that highlight the importance of education are:

- "Knowledge enables the possessor to distinguish right from wrong; it lights the way to Heaven; it is our friend in the desert, our society in solitude, our companion when friendless; it guides us to happiness; it sustains us in misery, it is our ornament amongst friends and an armour against enemies."
- "Studying is like glorifying God, and teaching is like charity."
- "Learn, teach and widen your knowledge and do not die ignorant. God does not excuse ignorance."
- "To the student who goes forth in search of knowledge, God allots a high place in the mansions of bliss; every lesson received has its rewards."
- "The ink of the scholar is more holy than the blood of the martyr."

Islam does not excuse those who have no desire to learn and upgrade themselves. The Qur'an addresses such people in very forceful terms as follows:

- "Those who do not observe, listen and understand are like cattle." (7:179)
- "Those who are blind in this world will be blind in the Hereafter." (17:72)

Muslim women too have the same privilege in education as the men. The Prophet said: "The acquisition of knowledge is the obligation of every Muslim, male or female."

The Prophet also put emphasis on lifelong learning. He advised: "Seek knowledge from the cradle to the grave."

INFORMAL LEARNING

People learn a lot by travelling and visiting other countries. They learn from what they observe of the environment, both natural and man-made, and through interaction with others. Through this globalisation process, they learn about other people's expertise and cultures, among other numerous learning points.

Human beings, who started from a pair of parents, have spread throughout the world and therefore ought to keep in contact with one another to broaden their knowledge and mind and become more interactive and tolerant. God says: "O mankind! We created you from a single pair of male and female, and made you into nations and tribes (races) so that you may know each other." (49:13)

The importance and benefits of globalisation in education was already realised more than 14 centuries ago. Today, it has become a norm for institutions of learning in advanced countries to implement global education schemes for their students. These schemes incorporate student exchanges, attachments, participative and educational visit programmes to provide added value to the in-campus acquisition of knowledge and skills.

Another Islamic motivator of informal learning is the Haj, the annual Islamic pilgrimage. Muslims have to travel to Mecca, a place where pilgrims of diverse races and cultures from all over the world assemble to perform their religious obligations. The Qur'an, in emphasising the learning factor of the Haj, indicates that pilgrims "may learn things that are of benefit to them" (22:28).

God also urges man to enjoy and learn from the natural environment, especially from the natural features of the earth and human survival endeavours. God says that He "has made the earth manageable for you, so travel and enjoy what God has provided for your sustenance" (67:15). "Sustenance" includes everything man needs to live, including the opportunities to learn and obtain anything profitable, and making contacts and dealings for trade, business and tourism.

In their own countries, people take things for granted; they "open their eyes" wider only when they travel. Thus, God says: "Travel through the earth and see how God did originate creation." (29:20) Creation means both natural creations such as the special features of the earth, the animal kingdom, vegetation and human beings themselves, as well as man-made structures.

Natural creations include the Grand Canyon and the Niagara Falls in America, the Great Barrier Reef of Australia, the Fjords of Norway, the Himalayas in India and innumerable natural wonders everywhere on earth. All these are for man to see, wonder and to learn from. The believers would also come closer to God — for it is He who created these wonders and substances, by which people learn and use the knowledge acquired to build wonderful structures.

Man-made structures are numerous. The Taj Mahal in India is an excellent example. When people look at this splendid monument, they would certainly marvel at it for two main reasons: one, man's ingenuity in building such a complex building at that time; and two, the beautiful materials that were used in its construction, notably marble which came from the mountains of India and some other countries.

Knowledge for any development, even self-development, is abundantly available all around us. Those who do not use it or use their reason, especially in matters of religion, are like beasts of burden that carry learning and wisdom on their backs but do not understand or profit from it. The Qur'an likens such people as "a donkey laden with books" (62:5).

REASONING

The Qur'an lays great stress on pondering, thinking and rationalising, drawing attention to every aspect of God's creation and encouraging people to use their mind in their daily activities.

Numerous verses in the Qur'an end with phrases that motivate people to think. A few of them are:

- "... if only they could understand." (9:81)
- "... people who care to understand." (29:35)
- "... if they only knew." (39:26)
- "... in that are signs for those who reflect." (45:13)

Two of the many verses by which God asks people to observe and use their reason are:

- "... behold in the rain which God sends down from the skies ... in the creatures of all kinds that He causes to multiply ... in the change of winds and the clouds ... in all these are signs indeed for people who use their reason." (2:164)
- "And your Lord taught the bee to build its cells in hills, on trees, and in men's habitation; ... there issues from within their (the bees') bodies a drink of varying colours; wherein is healing for men. Verily in this is a sign for those who give thought." (16:68–69)

The Qur'an pays special attention to building and developing man's intellectual capability by encouraging inquiry and logical argument. For instance, God quotes Prophet Abraham questioning his father who worshipped idols, thus: "Dear father! Why do you worship those things which hear not and see not, nor can they profit you anything?" (19:42)

And again, using a similar style of argument, concerning Moses' people, God says: "The people of Moses made in his absence, out of their ornaments, the image of a calf for worship: did they not see that it could neither speak to them, nor show them the (Straight) Way (the Way of God)?" (7:148) In a very forceful way, God says: "Those who do not observe, listen and understand are like cattle." (7:179) and as a follow-up, Prophet Muhammad advised: "God has given man as a guide, his reason; then use it in respect of all things and God's blessings will always guide you right."

SCIENCE

Islam encourages the learning of any useful knowledge, including science, for the progress of humanity. Here are some examples of the Prophet's sayings that provide motivation and encouragement for studies and research in the sciences:

- "To listen to the instructions of science and learning for one hour is more meritorious than attending the funeral of a thousand martyrs."
- "One hour's study of the creations of God is worth more than ten years of ignorant prayers."
- "For every disease there is a cure."

In encouraging scientific studies and research, the Qur'an mentions a number of scientific facts that were unknown to the world then. Here are a few of them:

- "The moon has no light of its own and that what we see is the reflected light of the sun." (91:1–2)
- "The universe came about by a big bang or disintegration billions of years ago." (21:30)
- "The reproduction of a life in the womb goes through various stages." (22:5)
- "All celestial bodies, such as the moon and planets, have their own course of orbit." (7:54 & 21:33)
- "There is also life (in whatever form) in other parts of the universe." (42:29)
- "Space travel is possible with knowledge." (55:33)

The Qur'an makes frequent references to the natural phenomena of the universe as incentives for scientific investigations and research, such as:

- "Do they not observe the birds, held poised in the midst of the air and the sky?" (16:79)
- "Don't you see how God makes the clouds move gently, then joins them together, then makes them into a heap? Then you see the rain pouring from their midst … Verily in these things is an instructive example for those who have vision." (24:43–44)
- "Do they not look at the camels, how they are created? And at the sky, how it is raised high? And at the earth, how it is spread out?" (88:17–20)

In another part of the Qur'an, a similar pointer as given in 16:79 is shown thus: "Do they not observe the birds and see how they fly?" (67:19) Such motivators gave man the idea to study aerodynamics, and so, centuries later, aeroplanes were built, and the progress continues with bigger and speedier aeroplanes and other aircraft.

Space travel is also alluded to in the Qur'an. Today, with (scientific) knowledge, man has made space travel possible. But how far can man travel in outer space? God says: "If you can pass beyond the zones of the heavens and the earth, pass you! You shall not be able to pass without authority." (55:33) Muslim scholars, apart from its religious rendering, have also given this verse a scientific interpretation. They point out that the phrase "without authority" means "without the power of knowledge". Hence, as man continues to attain advanced knowledge in the science of spacecraft and space travel, he would be able to go further into space to reach the planets, penetrating "beyond the zones of the heavens and the earth".

Any scientific knowledge that helps in the growth of human civilisation is hailed by Islam.

17 ▲ "SIGNS" OF GOD

Muslims believe in the miracles of God, for all humans to notice and ponder over. The Qur'an indicates two main types of miracles: one, those that happen naturally, termed in the Qur'an as "Signs of God"; and the other, those that were performed by the prophets of God (with God's authority).

God's help to individuals in times of their need, seen as miracles by them, do happen anytime to any individual whether he believes in God (through his religion) or not. This often happens as a result of intense prayer or heartfelt imploration of divine help in times of great despair or a dire misfortune. This is a direct help from God to all human beings, irrespective of their religious beliefs. The Qur'an says: "The help of God is always near (to all)." (2:214)

NATURAL MIRACLES
Many natural miracles or "Signs of God" are mentioned in the Qur'an. The two well-known ones are the Spring of Zamzam and the birth of Jesus Christ.

The Spring of Zamzam
When Hagar, the second wife of Prophet Abraham, having depleted her supply of water, placed her infant (Ishmael) at a spot in a desert and ran to look for passing caravans for help, water suddenly began to flow out from the parched, sun-baked land near the baby. Hagar was saved from dying of thirst, and the nourishment she received from drinking the water saved baby Ishmael who grew up to be a prophet himself. The spring, known as the Well of Zamzam, has been issuing water ever since.

Not only Hagar had drunk this water but also Prophet Abraham, Prophet Ishmael and Prophet Muhammad. Also, billions of Haj and Umrah pilgrims throughout the ages have drunk it. What is more, billions of people residing in the four corners of the world who had never visited Mecca have also drunk the water — given to them by returning pilgrims who had brought it with them in special containers ever since the Haj was instituted. This miracle stays right to this day.

In a way, the Zamzam water is a miracle water, but it is not regarded as holy water that can cure diseases, for instance. Islam does not ask people to believe in miracles as an easy way out of a problem or a bad situation. A combination of faith (trust) in God as well as action (work) to achieve or to solve problems is what Islam advocates.

The Birth of Jesus Christ

When the angels told Mary that she would conceive Jesus, she was shocked as she was an unmarried pious woman. She exclaimed: "O My Lord! How shall I have a son when no man has touched me? God said: 'Even so God creates what He wills. When He has decreed a Plan, He but says 'Be' and it is." (3:47)

Explaining that this was possible with God's Power, the Qur'an points out, as a contrast, that a greater miracle happened with Prophet Adam — he was created not only without a father but also without a mother: "The similitude of Jesus before God is that of Adam; He (God) created him from dust, then said to him 'Be' and he was." (3:59)

MIRACLES OF PROPHETS

Prophets had also performed miracles, as directed by God, to convince their people of their respective missions.

Prophet Moses and Jesus Christ were well known for having performed miracles. Some of their miracles mentioned in the Qur'an are as follows:

- Prophet Moses parted the Red Sea.
  "The Pharaoh led his people astray instead of leading them aright." (22:79). And when Prophet Moses attempted to make Pharoah realise that he was no god and urged him to surrender to the true God, he (Pharaoh) wanted to annihilate him and his followers. But God "sent an inspiration to Moses" asking him

and his followers to cross the "sea without fear", as it parted, to escape from the pursuing solders.

• Jesus Christ performed various miracles.
God says that Jesus Christ performed miracles "by My leave", meaning by God's permission or authority. The miracles included making a bird out of clay, healing those born blind, healing the lepers, and giving life to the dead. (5:113)

THE MIRACULOUS "NIGHT JOURNEY"

Prophet Muhammad, who was sent by God "as a Mercy for mankind" (21:107), was the only prophet to have ascended to Heaven and returned. Upon his return, he related his experiences to his followers and emphasised the reality of Heaven and Hell, and taught Muslims the *solat* which Muslims throughout the world perform five times a day right to this day.

The Prophet's ascension to Heaven took place on 27 Rejab, the seventh month of the Hijrah (Muslim) calendar. The event, called "Isra' Mi'raj" or "The Night Journey", is mentioned in Chapter 17 of the Qur'an. This spiritual journey comprises two parts — Isra' and Mi'raj.

Isra' is Prophet Muhammad's land journey from the Ka'aba in Mecca to Masjidil Aqsa (the "Farthest Mosque") in Jerusalem. Masjidil Aqsa or Baitul Maqdis includes the present-day gold-coloured Dome of the Rock which is also known as the Mosque of Omar. Before Islam, this was a "temple" — a place for the worship of God, known in Islam as the "Farthest Mosque". It was first frequented by Prophet Abraham.

Mi'raj is the Prophet's journey from earth, from Masjidil Aqsa to Heaven. ("Heaven" means the spiritual Heaven and not the physical "heavens" which refers to the universe.)

According to the Hadith, Prophet Muhammad was sleeping near the Ka'aba when he was approached by the Archangel Gabriel who informed the Prophet that he had been invited by God to visit Heaven that very night.

The Prophet, accompanied by the Archangel Gabriel, went on a vehicle described as a winged steed, called *Buraaq*. During the journey to Masjidil Aqsa, he saw many visions; and during his ascent to Heaven, he met a number of prophets, including Prophet Adam, Prophet Moses and Jesus Christ. When he reached the highest (seventh) level of the Heaven, Sidratul Muntaha, he felt the presence of God.

On the way back from Sidratul Muntaha, the Prophet again travelled through the seven levels of Heaven, witnessing the happenings in Paradise and Hell as he descended to earth. Then, from Masjidil Aqsa to the Ka'aba, the Prophet again saw certain visions, all of which are described in detail in the Hadith.

Readers need to be aware that whatever the Prophet saw during the "Night Journey" (as described in the Hadith) are all to be taken in the spiritual sense as they are metaphorically expressed for common understanding, just as "Gardens" is a metaphorical expression for Paradise and "Fire" for Hell. Although God does not require a vehicle to be sent to the Prophet to fetch him because, according to the Qur'an, God need only say "Be" and it happens, in this case a unique creature called *Buraaq* is mentioned. This vehicle was mentioned merely for human understanding. *Buraaq*, in today's computer age, could simply stand for speed.

But, even with the allegory of *Buraaq*, when the Prophet told the Meccans about his Isra' and Mi'raj experiences, many were doubtful about the story. How could a person travel from Mecca to Jerusalem in just one night when normally such a journey on camel would take two months, they argued.

Some even asked the Prophet for proof. A man who had been to the Jerusalem "temple" (as it was referred to before Islam) asked the Prophet to describe it, which the Prophet did to the inquirer's satisfaction. Another asked if the Prophet had seen anything on his way back to Mecca and the Prophet said he saw a *qafilah* (a caravan consisting of a group of tradesmen with their camels) heading towards Mecca which should arrive within the next 24 hours. The Prophet described the caravan, even saying that the tradesmen had lost a camel. The caravan did arrive, as related by the Prophet, with the other details clearly matched.

The people of Mecca of that time and era could be excused for wondering how it could be possible to make a return journey to Jerusalem in just one night. This is surely not impossible with today's air travel "miracles" such as jets and rocket-propelled vehicles. And wouldn't air travel be even faster in the future?

Thus, the *Buraaq* should be seen as an indication of the advancement of long-distance transportation and communication with sophisticated vehicles and facilities of today and in time to come with emphasis on speed.

Just as a traveller who goes to a faraway land would be happy to bring home special gifts for loved ones awaiting his return, Prophet Muhammad too returned from his miraculous journey with a very special gift for his followers. In fact, the special gift was from God to the believers. It is the *solat*.

Indeed the *solat* is one of the greatest blessings of God. It gives the Muslim the opportunity "to ascend" and get closer to his Creator when he performs it earnestly. The *solat* is the Mi'raj for Muslims.

PROPHET MUHAMMAD'S "MIRACLES"
Islamic traditions mention that Prophet Muhammad had performed a number of miracles for specific purposes. But Muslims do not highlight them in order to believe in him as the final Prophet sent by God to deliver the final testament, the Qur'an.

During the Prophet's time, many of the pagan Meccans had asked the Prophet to perform miracles so that they could believe in his teachings, but he would always say (as instructed by God): "I am only a warner and bringer of glad tidings to those who believe" (7:188) and that miracles as performed by some of the earlier prophets to convince people of their missions were of no use in his (modern) time.

When still pressed for miracles by some people, the Prophet would just say (in a metaphorical sense): "The Qur'an is my miracle."

Indeed the Qur'an is a living miracle, one as seen by the Prophet himself and existing right to this day in the hands of Muslims, but as the Prophet himself had advised, the miracle of the Qur'an would work when it is read regularly and its wisdom put into practice.

18 🕌 RELATIONSHIP WITH NON-MUSLIMS

Certain Islamic beliefs, practices and virtues are almost similar to those of other religions because Divine Messages come from the same One God. As such, common basic or fundamental truths like morals and virtues are found in all religions, more so in Judaism, Christianity and Islam as they share the same ancestral roots: the "father" of these three great religions is Prophet Abraham.

Islam teaches Muslims to establish closeness with people of any religion, even those without any faith, to learn from them in whatever good they can offer. For this reason, Prophet Muhammad said: "Go even to China in search of knowledge." This he said because the Chinese were culturally superior to many communities in the world at that time. There is no discrimination in Islam over race, colour, culture or faith. Islam teaches Muslims to enhance cordial relationship with non-Muslims for any good cause.

"PEOPLE OF THE BOOK"

There are many similarities in the beliefs and practices among the people of the Semitic religions — Judaism, Christianity and Islam. Islam refers to them as "People of the Book" (5:16) because they have been given guidance and instructions by God through (His) Revelations: Prophet Moses received the *Taurat* or Torah (the Law); Jesus Christ, the *Injil* or Gospel (Good News); and Prophet Muhammad, the Qur'an (the Message).

Each of these Revelations contains guidance on worldly and spiritual matters. The Law contains "guidance and light" (5:47), so does the Gospel (5:49). As the Religion of God has been delivered by the various prophets in developmental or progressive stages, from the basic to the more comprehensive, certain basic beliefs and practices are therefore the common factors among the "People of the Book".

Prophet Moses taught the oneness of God, morals and righteousness as well as spiritual attainment. Jesus Christ came and confirmed the Law (5:49), meaning he instructed his people to carry on practising the teachings of the Law (delivered by Prophet Moses) and delved more on spiritual matters. When Prophet Muhammad came, he too confirmed the Law of Prophet Moses and the Gospel of Jesus Christ (5:51) — and went a step further. In matters of prayer and fasting, for instance, as Islam had come as the final stage of development of the Religion of God, he showed people when and how the *solat* is to be performed, and when and how fasting is to be conducted. Thus the *solat* and fasting became formalised, standardised and obligatory in Islam.

Here are some other similarities:

- Islam makes it an article of the Islamic faith to believe in all prophets of God, including Prophet Adam (the first of more than 124,000 prophets), Prophet Abraham, Prophet Ishmael, Prophet Isaac, Prophet Noah, Prophet Moses, John the Baptist and Jesus Christ (the penultimate prophet before Prophet Muhammad).
- Male Muslims are circumcised just like the male followers of Judaism.
- For food, followers of Judaism slaughter animals as Muslims do. With Jews, the meat is call *kosher* while in Islam it is called *halal*, both terms meaning permissible for consumption. This food law allows Muslims to eat *kosher* products which also needs certification to sell.
- Pork is also *haram* in Judaism just as it is in Islam.
- The followers of Judaism offer "*Shalom*" (Peace) as their greeting. The Arabic equivalent is "*Salam*", and Muslims greet one another by saying, "*Assalamu-alaikum*" (Peace be on you).
- There are many Muslim names similar to those of the followers of Judaism and Christianity, such as Aaron, Daniel, Isabelle and Sharon.

Addressing the "People of the Book" (3:99), God urges them to come together and work for the benefit of humanity: "Let there arise out of you a band of people inviting to all that is good, enjoining what is right, and forbidding what is wrong: they are the ones to attain felicity. Be not like those who are divided amongst themselves and fall into disputations after receiving Clear Signs (from God)." (3:104–105)

INTERACTION WITH NON-MUSLIMS

Communication builds and strengthens relationships and friendships. Going to the mosque to perform the *solat* instead of performing it alone at home is an example. Going for the Haj is another example. Visiting people on Eid ul-Fitri (Festival of Charity) is yet another. All these are practices of "good works" or social skills that enable Muslims to make friends and renew friendship among Muslims. Since Muslims already possess such social "skills", they should have no problem interacting with non-Muslims to build close rapport with them.

Islam encourages Muslims to be friendly with and helpful to both Muslims and non-Muslims to promote fraternity and friendship. There are numerous sayings of Prophet Muhammad that point to the importance of strengthening social bonds between Muslims and non-Muslims. Some of them are:

- "Treat kindly the dwellers of the earth (all living creatures) and God will treat you kindly."
- "God says: 'If you wish to receive graciousness from Me, show graciousness to those whom I have created.'" (The "created" also includes animals and other creatures and pets.)
- "He who for the sake of God loves another human being, that person verily has extolled the glory of God."
- "God says: 'Love becomes obligatory on My part for those who on My sake love one another and live together and who for my sake greet each other with a goodly cheer and who on My sake spend of what they earn for the good of one another.'"

And God says: "Whoever saves a life, it is as though he had saved the lives of all men." (5:35)

God allowed different communities to flourish to provide them with the opportunity to do "good works" together. The Qur'an says: "If God had so willed, He would have made you all one single (religious) community; but (He willed it otherwise) in order to test you by whatever (revelation) He has given you. So strive you as in race with one another in all virtues and good works!" (5:51)

The above verse shows that Muslims are not to live apart or away from the non-Muslim community. God desires Muslims to work with people of other faiths and together do "good works" for the benefit of everyone and humanity as a whole.

Muslims and non-Muslims have much to learn from one another, and that is precisely why mankind has been allowed to develop differently. Addressing everyone, God says: "O mankind! We created you from a single pair of a male and a female, and made you into nations and tribes, that you may know each other." (49:13)

It would be for the benefit of a country when its Muslim and non-Muslim citizens "know one another" and work together for righteous living, which includes educational and employment opportunities, and harmonious relations among its citizens of all races and faiths. God commands all of us: "Help you one another in righteousness and piety, and do not co-operate with one another in sin and transgression." (5:3)

EATING WITH NON-MUSLIMS

Islam does not forbid Muslims from mixing and eating together with non-Muslims at the same table. Muslims take *halal* food as an instruction from God. Therefore, there is no problem for a Muslim to be eating *halal* food and sitting with a non-Muslim who is eating non-*halal* food like chicken or rice porridge that has minced pork as an ingredient.

However, a Muslim would avoid eating at the same table with his non-Muslim friends:

- if there is a whole or a big chunk of roasted pig displayed on the table or near the table where he sits. This is just a preference because of the strong smell from the roasted pig, which is alien to him, just as a Westerner may not feel comfortable if he sits near somebody eating durian, a fruit he is not used to.
- if they are taking alcoholic drinks because he (the Muslim) may be misconstrued as consuming alcohol too, as alcohol is prohibited to Muslims. The smell of beer and other alcoholic beverages may also be unpleasant to people who do not drink.

In Singapore, most non-Muslims are aware of the Muslim dietary preferences, and so for get-together functions, they often engage the services of Muslim caterers or non-Muslim caterers who have acquired the Halal Certificate issued by the Islamic Religious Council of Singapore (Muis) or dine at restaurants that have the Halal certificate.

ATTENDING NON-MUSLIM FUNCTIONS

Islam teaches Muslims to respect all religions.

A Muslim can visit the places of worship of non-Muslims, be it a church or a Chinese or Hindu temple. He may also attend weddings held in a church or temple. At all times, he must be respectful to the worshippers and remain quiet when the prayers are said.

It is not taboo for a Muslim to attend the funeral service of a non-Muslim to offer condolences and donations to the bereaved family. A Muslim must show respect even if he comes across a non-Muslim funeral procession of a person he does not know.

A Hadith records Prophet Muhammad as saying: "When you see a funeral procession (even that of a non-Muslim), you should stand up as a mark of respect." Another record mentions that the Prophet quickly took a standing position and commanded his companions to do likewise when the funeral bier of a Jew passed by. When questioned, the Prophet replied: "Has he not got a soul?" All Muslims and non-Muslims have been created by God. The Islamic spirit is that your friends, colleagues or neighbours who have lost their loved ones should be consoled and their grief shared.

The Hadith says "Whoever does not love human beings, God will not love him" and teaches Muslims to be friendly with neighbours irrespective of their faiths. And in the Qur'an, Muslims are taught not to be arrogant with anyone (31:18) and to help people who are in need irrespective of their faiths (107:1–7).

These are important pointers in establishing close bonds among people of various ethnic groups and religions. The Islamic message to one and all is: "Strive together (as in a competitive race) towards all that is good." (2:148)

19 ▲HUMAN FAILINGS

Islam is concerned with the uplifting of moral values and the upholding of justice, peace and righteousness and curtailing of wrongdoing. God says that He "enjoins justice and kindness and forbids indecency and abomination and wickedness." (16:90)

Babies (of parents of any race or religion) are born with *fitrah* (the state of purity and sinlessness) and they accumulate sins as they grow up by committing offences (impiety and wrongdoings) through temptation, ignorance, egoism or pride. In the sublime language of the Qur'an, they "have transgressed against their souls" (39:53). Islam teaches Muslims to focus on Islamic righteousness and practices to increase the purity of his soul. God says: "He shall indeed attain to a happy state who causes his soul to grow in purity. And truly lost is he who buries it (in darkness)." (91:7–10)

WRONGDOING

In Islam, each and every Muslim is answerable to God for his misbehaviour and wrongdoings.

The conduct of a Muslim is governed by basic principles of *halal* and *haram*. These are meant to guide a person in developing an upright Islamic character and behaviour. So, when a Muslim flouts an Islamic rule, say gambling or drinking alcohol which are *haram* activities, he has committed a wrongdoing. What is more, when he gambles or drinks alcohol, he would most certainly not be performing his *solat* and fast in Ramadan. Such a person may not have been brought up Islamically due to some family circumstances, and so is ignorant of Islam. A wrongdoing stems not only from ignorance but also from greed, temptations, hatred, influences and other reasons.

In some Muslim communities, child marriages, selling off one's daughters for want of money and suppression of women are practised. These are pre-Islamic practices, now deemed un-Islamic. Muslims who indulge in superstitions and deviant practices have also deviated from the "straight path". All these are wrongdoings.

Groups or individuals involved in acts of terrorism and violence that result in the deaths of innocent people and the destruction of public properties in the name of Islam are not upholding Islamic principles. Nothing in Islamic teachings defends any activity generally regarded as terrorism, a present-day term that comes under the Qur'anic phrase "evil" or "mischief on earth". God points these out in numerous ways throughout the Qur'an such as:

- "Eat and drink of the subsistence provided by God but do no evil nor mischief on the (face of the) earth." (2:60)
- "Whoever recommends and helps a good cause becomes a partner therein and whoever recommends and helps an evil cause shares in its burden." (4:85)
- "Those who seek gain in evil, they are companions of the Fire. But those who have faith and work righteousness, they are companions of the Gardens." (2:81–82)
- "Evil is hateful in the sight of God." (17:38)

God advises people to spend their wealth for good causes, and not on activities that cause distress, destruction and death. The Qur'an says: "And spend of your substance in the cause of God, and make not your own hands contribute to (your) destruction. But do good, for God loves those who do good." (2:195)

In Islam, instead of begging to make a living, any job undertaken to support a livelihood is considered as "doing good", hence it constitutes *ibadah*. To work as an engineer, a doctor, a clerk or a road cleaner is *ibadah*. However, if the clerk manipulates the financial records of his employer and misappropriates some of the funds, the action is unrighteous and does not constitute *ibadah*. Similarly, for a man to marry and have children is *ibadah* but when he abuses his own children (say, incest), it is not *ibadah*. Such wrongdoings are serious as they affect other people and so the guilty parties will have to face appropriate punishment.

Personal and communal wrongdoings

Wrongdoings are divided into two broad areas — personal and communal. A personal sin is the consequence of a wrongdoing committed against God's command, and a communal sin is one for a wrongdoing committed against human beings.

A person who commits a personal wrongdoing, for instance not fasting in the month of Ramadan or not performing the daily *solat*, accumulates sins. Only God knows why the person commits a particular sin and how grave the sin is. Only God "knows all things" (5:57). So, He is the Judge of personal sins.

Communal wrongdoings include the committing of crimes such as theft, rape, murder, destruction, terrorism and other atrocities that harm the individual, the society, as well as the environment. For a wrongdoing like theft or rape, the punishment (according to Islamic or secular law) is meted out. Those who escape from being punished on earth altogether or punished inadequately will be dealt with accordingly in the Hereafter. God says "They hide (their crimes) from men, but they cannot hide (them) from God ..." (4:108)

PUNISHMENT

When a wrongdoer is caught, he is punished. God says:

- "Whoever works evil will be punished accordingly (with justice) ..." (4:123)
- "... and those who commit injustice and wrongdoing on earth shall be punished." (26:227)

When a wrongdoer escapes (earthly) punishment, he would not be able to escape punishment in the Hereafter for his wrongdoing or sin. A sin is a blemish on the soul of the wrongdoer. It is a spiritual demerit point. For instance, when a man is caught for torturing and mutilating a cat, his wrongdoing is punished by the law of the country. If nobody saw the cruel act and the culprit is not caught, he still sins. Sins are accumulated and the wrongdoer receives the punishment in the Hereafter.

Just as humans are able to record words, pictures and sounds by electronic means, every good or bad action of a person is recorded through Godly means and given the merit or demerit points accordingly.

Any action — bad or good — however small, is accounted for to mete out divine justice.

Punishments, whether imposed by the Shari'ah or secular law, are meted out (with justice) for the general well-being of the whole community and nation.

Theft is a popular crime since time immemorial. In Islam, the punishment for theft comes under a section of the Islamic law called *hudud* (punishment rules). *Hudud* is based on justice, fairness, compassion, and, at the same time, strictness, as *hudud* looks at the deterrence factor for the general good of everybody in the whole (Islamic) country. Under *hudud*, no offender would lose an arm for stealing a loaf of bread but he would surely be counselled or punished for it in some way.

The focus in *hudud* is prevention. Therefore, the punishment must carry sufficient weight to ensure that the culprit would not commit any crime again and again. Other *hudud* penalties for adultery, fornication and sexual indulgence that could tear apart the social fabric of the family or society, and which can result in broken marriages, sexually transmitted diseases and AIDS, are all meant for righteous and gracious living and for the good of everyone in the country.

Hudud looks at justice, and so punishments are meted out according to the severity of the crime. God says: "... if any does evil, the doers of evil are only punished (to the extent) of their deeds." (28:84)

Killing of people is *haram* and is a serious crime. The punishment for killings resulting from acts of terrorism is very severe, both in this world and in the next.

God says: "The punishment ... for mischief through the land is execution ... or exile from the land. That is their disgrace in this world, and a heavy punishment is theirs in the Hereafter." (5:36)

Describing the severity of killing innocent people, God says: "Whoever kills a person — unless it be for murder or for spreading mischief in the land (which will be dealt with by the authorities) — it is as if he had killed all mankind." (5:32)

God has given ample warnings on wrongdoings. To those who knowingly ignore them, or misinterpret Qur'anic verses to serve their own interest, God says: "They have hearts with which they understand not (the truth), eyes with which they see not, and ears with which they hear not. They are like cattle — nay, more misguided: for they are heedless of warnings." (7:179)

God advises people to be righteous always. The Qur'an says: "In the end, it is to God that you shall be brought back." (39:44) With this in mind, an Islamic teaching point states: Since we came from God in a pure and sinless state, would we not be ashamed to return to Him in a terribly impure state with a soul shockingly defiled?

The followers of Islam are not called Muhammadans because they do not worship Prophet Muhammad who was created by God. They worship God alone, hence they are called Muslims ("one who submits to God"), a term mentioned in the Qur'an itself.

Islam introduced a concept of togetherness known as the *ummah* (global community of Muslims). It embraces all Muslims of the world, taking them as members of a huge global family.

Racial barriers do not exist in Islam. Every Muslim is a brother to another, regardless of his race or colour or from whichever corner of the globe he hails from. Every Muslim is part of this well-balanced, borderless *ummah*, a global Islamic fraternity based on religious solidarity. God says: "We have made you an *ummah* justly balanced." (2:143)

THE ISLAMIC CREED

The *Shahadah*, the first of the Five Pillars of Islam, is a testimony of acceptance to be a Muslim. It is a short declaration that goes: "*Ash hadu Allah illaha illallah, wa ash hadu anna Muhammadur Rasullullah*" (I bear witness that there is no god except God (Allah) and that Muhammad is the Messenger of God).

The testimony finds support in the Qur'an: "Obey God and the Messenger, that you may obtain mercy." (3:132)

An intending convert to Islam is required to pronounce it in the presence of at least one witness to become a Muslim. A conversion certificate is not required but it is good to obtain one to prove that one is a Muslim to enter Mecca when intending to perform the Haj or Umrah as non-Muslims are not allowed to enter the Holy Land.

In Singapore all conversion centres issue the certificate immediately upon conversion.

Born Muslims need not say the testimony before witnesses because they would have pronounced it countless times in their lifetime during the *solat*, and God is the witness.

The *Shahadah* comprises two parts: the first is the belief in the Oneness of God, and the other is the belief in the prophethood of Muhammad. A close scrutiny of the first part of the *Shahadah* shows that it contains two sections: one, a negation — that there is no god (with a lower case "g"); and the other, an affirmation — that there is Allah (commonly referred to in English as God with a capital "G"). By declaring that there is no god, the Muslim is, in fact, saying that he worships no sun, fire, idols, saints, ancestors, royalty or even prophets. Instead, he worships Allah — the One and Only God, "Lord and Cherisher of all the worlds" (45:36).

The second part of the *Shahadah* stresses the importance of Prophet Muhammad as the final prophet. God says that He sent him "as a Witness, a Bearer of Glad Tidings and a Warner" (33:45).

The *Shahadah* is actually the Islamic creed: "There is no god but God. Muhammad is the Messenger of God" which Muslim flags, emblems and wall-decorations carry in stunning Arabic calligraphic forms.

CONCEPT OF "MUSLIM"

"Muslim" is a word used in the Qur'an to refer to a person who totally surrenders or submits himself to God alone and does not regard any deity or human being as God or god-incarnate. In this sense, all prophets of God before Islam, including Prophet Abraham, Prophet Moses and Prophet Jesus (Jesus Christ), were Muslims because they worshipped none but God and taught their followers the essence of Islam: "Serve God and eschew evil." (16:36)

"Muslim" is neither a race nor people of one race. Muslims are people of many races bound together by a universal code of brotherhood. In Singapore and Malaysia, almost all Malays are Muslims. In these two multi-racial, multi-religious countries, there are Muslims among the non-Malays too. There are Indian Muslims, Chinese Muslims, Indonesian Muslims and others. Muslims are found in all ethnic groups and nationalities in the world. There are American Muslims (both

Caucasian and Black), European Muslims, Middle-Eastern Muslims, African Muslims, Indonesian Muslims, Indian Muslims (in India) and Chinese Muslims (in China), and others, including Korean, Japanese and Filipino Muslims.

In general, a Muslim is one whose religion is Islam. A Muslim serves God, and serving God means following the commands of God, which include "eschewing evil" (16:36), "doing good and refraining from wrong" (3:172) and practising Islamic virtues (33:35).

MUSLIM IDENTITY
A righteous or "total" Muslim is one who combines his religious practices with good intentions, modest speech and righteous acts. Generally, he:

* has a correct understanding of Islam.
* exercises Islamic virtues like responsibility, humility, perseverance, honesty, integrity, neighbourliness, and strives to improve his general well-being and goodwill.
* respects and loves all human beings, irrespective of race and religion.
* performs his *solat*.
* fasts in Ramadan.
* gives *zakat*.
* eats only *halal* food.
* does not drink or gamble (as these are prohibited in Islam).
* observes modesty in the way he/she dresses and speaks.
* cultivates purity (through cleanliness, keeping away from pre-marital sex, avoiding negative influences, etc).
* makes sure that he does not get involved in wrongdoings such as sexual offences, theft, terrorism, violence and killings.

A Muslim who drinks or gambles and does not care about *halal* food would also surely not observe the more difficult Islamic practices such as performing the *solat* and fasting in Ramadan. He is a person with a Muslim name only. In fact, he is very far away from Islam and certainly cannot be identified as a Muslim.

Muslims who do not have a correct understanding of Islam, or are "hypocrites", intentionally or unintentionally tarnish the good name of Islam. They may follow a so-called religious leader blindly no matter how absurd the leader's teachings. Many such leaders, charismatic in personality and affable in speech, have come and gone in shame. Often the members of fanatical groups follow only one religious teacher. Islam however urges Muslims to learn Islam from various sources so as to be broadminded in their *Deen*, the believers' way of life.

A righteous or "total" Muslim would follow the (real) teachings of Islam and would certainly not leave, or be indifferent to, a religion that is "comprehensive and complete" (5:4).

MUSLIM NAMES

There are many Muslim names that appear similar to Christian names. This is because Islam, Christianity and Judaism are all Semitic religions, historically coming from the same religious line, from Prophet Abraham.

Many Muslim names have a little variation to those of Christian names in spelling, for example, Dawood for David, Ishak for Isaac, Yusof for Joseph for males; and Mariam for Mary and Supiah for Sophia for females. For female names, the letter "h" may or may not be added to the end of the name, like Dianah for Diana, Ameliah for Amelia and Sabrinah for Sabrina.

Some male Muslim names, such as Adam, Benjamin, Martin and Daniel, are exactly the same as Christian names. Female Muslim names, such as Alicia, Sarah and Sharon, are the same as Christian names.

Many male Muslim names take after the attributes of God, for example Rahman which means "the Merciful". Hence, "Abdul" which means "servant of" is added to the name. Thus, Abdul Rahman means "Servant of the Merciful". In Singapore, it is a common practice for a convert to add the Muslim name Abdullah, meaning "servant of Allah", to his name.

Nur or Noor is a popular forename. "Nur" or "Noor" means "guidance" or "light". Thus, Noor Muhammad (male name) means Guidance or Light of (Prophet) Muhammad and Nur Ain Saleha (female name) means Light of the eyes of a pious person.

When a man converts to Islam, it may be necessary for him to adopt a Muslim name. This is just for official documentation purposes. For instance, only Muslims are allowed entry into Mecca, say, to perform the Haj or Umrah. Therefore, an official document is required to show that the person intending to enter Mecca is a Muslim.

Some converts use their Muslim names and their original names separately while some others use their Muslim names together with their surnames. A few examples of names of converts (taken from various issues of *The Muslim Reader*, a quarterly magazine of The Muslim Converts' Association of Singapore) are: Norashikin Abdullah alias Lim Ai Lin and Murliani Abdullah alias Janet See Kim Gek, Mazlan Abdullah Soh, Siti Aminah Han and Adam Abdullah Brown (the last three persons have retained their Chinese/English surnames).

Although a Muslim convert has a Muslim name, he or she may continue using his or her former name. One such person is Peter Augustine Goh, a well-known Chinese personality who regularly contributes articles on Islam and short stories to the local Malay newspapers using his former name in the byline. Malaysian TV personality and newscaster Peggie Ng retains her name in the credits, and her colleagues call her "Peggie".

Muslims are discouraged from having distasteful names. For example, "Ah Kow", which means "dog" in a Chinese dialect, would not be retained by a Chinese man with such a name when he becomes a Muslim. Cat Stevens, the British pop idol of the 1960s, when he embraced Islam adopted the name "Yusuf Islam" without retaining his former name "Cat". Muhammad Ali, the all-time boxing great, dropped his former name, Cassius Clay, altogether. The well-known author of Islamic books Margaret Marcus became Maryam Jamilah. A convert is free to adopt any meaningful Islamic name of his or her choice.

In Islam, married Muslim women are encouraged to use their maiden names instead of taking their husbands' names. It is a right given to Muslim women by Islam. Miss Fatimah Ali (or Miss Fatimah binti Ali) means Fatimah is the daughter of Ali. Thus, if Miss Fatimah Ali marries Kassim bin Ahmad (Kassim son of Ahmad), she might not prefer to be addressed as Mrs Kassim or Mrs Fatimah Kassim or even Mrs Kassim-Fatimah Ali. She would prefer to be addressed by her maiden name: Madam Fatimah Ali or Ms Fatimah Ali.

CONVERSION TO ISLAM

A person of any race, culture, background or status can become a Muslim at any age in his/her life. He/she embraces Islam for two main reasons: (1) attraction to Islam and (2) marriage to a Muslim.

Among the people who embraced Islam because of its beauty is Ms Ruqaiyyah Waris Maqsood, formerly Rosalyn Rushbrook. A respected British author and educator, she says in her book *What Every Christian Should Know About Islam*: "I became Muslim because I discovered the real teachings of Islam."

Under the Shari'ah, parties intending marriage must be Muslims. Thus, for example, if a Buddhist Chinese man is going to marry a Muslim woman, he has to convert to Islam first.

Converting to Islam is not converting to a race, which is impossible. The convert also need not abandon his culture. A Chinese convert can still take part in such festivals as the Chinese New Year, the Lantern Festival and Chingay as long as any part of the festival does not contradict the teachings of Islam. He can visit his non-Muslim parents any time and on festive occasions like the Chinese New Year, and even join them in the reunion dinner; but he would eat only *halal* food, specially cooked or bought for him (and his wife, if he is married) for the dinner. He need not abandon his parents, family ties, community and heritage. If he is not living with his non-Muslim parents, he should invite them and his relatives to his home for any occasion or for the Eid ul-Fitri and Eid ul-Adha celebrations.

The race and culture of the persons intending marriage are not a concern in Islam because Islam advances the concept of *ummah* (Islamic brotherhood that embraces the world's multi-racial and multi-cultural Muslims as a family). Indeed the marriage of two people of different races and cultures are encouraged in Islam as such marriages would make the respective families "know", that is, learn more from one another and so enrich cultures and promote harmony and closeness among them.

God says: "O mankind! We created you and made you into nations and tribes (different races with varied cultures) so that you may know each other." (49:13)

Many non-Muslims who convert to Islam nowadays prefer to call themselves "Reverts" instead of "Converts". This is because "convert" means changing from a former religion to Islam while "revert" signifies returning to one's former nature, the situation when they were born — pure and innocent with an innate sense of submission to God — called the *fitrah*, the true characteristic of a Muslim. Prophet Muhammad said: "No child is born except upon *fitrah*. It is his parents who make him a Jew or a Christian or a polytheist."

Whether "convert" or "revert", the new believer in Islam ought to be happy as all his sins have been wiped out and he or she should try to attain that purity henceforth. God says: "Those to whom We sent the Book before this, they do believe in this (Qur'anic) Revelation. And when it is recited to them, they say: 'We believe therein, for it is the Truth from our Lord. Indeed we have been Muslims from before this'. Twice will they be given their reward, for they have persevered, and they avert evil with good, and they spend in charity out of what We have given them." (28:51–54)

However, referring to themselves as converts or reverts ought to be a short-term usage. The person who has become a Muslim must identify himself as a Muslim, and together with other Muslims strive towards peace in one's country of residence — in conforming to the name "Islam" which itself means "Peace upheld through total submission to God".

CONVERSION PROCESS

Conversion requirements may differ slightly from country to country. In Singapore, a conversion to Islam must be registered at the Islamic Religious Council of Singapore (Muis), the Singapore Muslim Missionary Society (Jamiyah) or the Muslim Converts' Association of Singapore (Darul Arqam). A person intending to embrace Islam has to observe certain rules and procedures as follows:

- The male must be at least 18 years old and the female at least 16.
- He/She officially converts to Islam (at any one of the above places) by pronouncing the *Shahadah*, the testimony of faith. The pledge is taken before at least two adult male Muslim witnesses. (Like a marriage, a secretive conversion is not encouraged. Witnesses and certification are required to avoid societal problems.)
- He/She takes a Muslim name for certification purposes only, so as to be permitted to enter Mecca to perfom the Haj or Umrah.
- He/She takes a basic course on Islam. It is desirable for him/her to attend the course (at any of the above-mentioned organisations) before the conversion.

The children of a family need not meet the age requirements if all the members in the family convert together.

SPIRIT OF ISLAMIC BROTHERHOOD

There is no caste system or colour superiority in Islam. All Muslims are brothers in Islam. An English, a Chinese, a French or an African-American who is a born Muslim or a convert to Islam is a brother to another Muslim who may be an Australian, an Indonesian, a Japanese or a Thai.

Muslims are bound and bonded together by religion. Once a person becomes a Muslim, he becomes a brother to all Muslims in the world. This was emphasised in the famous sermon of Prophet Muhammad, who delivered it during his Farewell Pilgrimage. The lead line on this aspect in the lengthy sermon reads: "No Arab has any superiority over a non-Arab. Muslims are but brothers to one another."

The significance of Islamic brotherhood is more evidently realised annually in the month of Zulhijjah, when some 2.5 million people of diverse races, cultures and traditions from various parts of the world gather in Mecca to perform the Haj and be part of the largest inter-racial gathering in the world.

In emphasising the spirit of brotherhood in Islam, Wilfried Hofmann, a German diplomat and convert to Islam, related his Haj experiences in his book *Journey to Islam*: "At the passport control, the young Saudi official studied, in turn, our pilgrims' visas and our faces, repeating this procedure enough times that I started to worry that something was not in bureaucratic order. Then, I noticed tears running down his face. Unexpectedly, he jumped up, leaned over the counter, and embraced me as a 'brother in Islam'."

21 🕌 UNIQUENESS OF ISLAM

Islam is a unique religion in that it has a law, the Shari'ah, which serves to protect and improve the lifestyle of Muslims.

Another uniqueness of Islam is that it prohibits superstition and any cultural or traditional practices that are un-Islamic, including fortune-telling, black magic and offerings to the dead. Also prohibited is the depiction of God in any form whether pictures or statues. It is also blasphemous to depict any Islamic prophets because they are highly respected, and any depiction of them would be a sheer mockery of their superior and pristine personalities.

Islam provides ample guidance to a person for his well-being in this world and preparation for the next, as well as flexibility in religious practices as not to overburden anyone. It informs him to be rational and clear-headed in all his daily worldly and spiritual responsibilities for the good of his own body, mind and soul.

ISLAMIC LAW

In Arabic, Islamic law is called the Shari'ah (spelt *syari'ah* in Malay). The main objective of the Shari'ah, which essence is derived from the Qur'an and the *Sunnah*, is to preserve and secure the general good and interests of Muslims and promote their welfare.

The Shari'ah's coverage is extensive. It contains laws for all aspects of living. Legal Islamic issues such as on divorces and family maintenance also come under the Shari'ah, and are handled by the Shari'ah Court.

New developments that are not directly mentioned in the Qur'an and the *Sunnah* are also dealt with under the Shari'ah. When a new development becomes an issue in a country, say for example organ donation, the country's scholars, headed by its *mufti* (official religious head), would exercise their reason and judgement to reach a legal decision after referring the subject or related subject in the Qur'an and the *Sunnah*. Such a consultation process, called *ijtihad*, is unique and specific for people of that country only, as the decision taken through *ijtihad* by Muslims of a country is not applicable to all Muslims in the world. The decision will have to be explained to the Muslims as a form of education before the *fatwa* (religious ruling) on the subject becomes part of the Shari'ah.

WAR AND ITS RULES

It is human nature to make mistakes of any kind, which can escalate to some level of disagreement or even serious conflict leading to a war.

Muslims are prohibited from being the aggressor or initiating unjust fighting. However, they are permitted to fight when they are oppressed, persecuted or attacked (4:75), even by other Muslims, "in the cause of God". Often referred to as jihad, it is undertaken in self-defence when all means for a peaceful resolution of the conflict do not go through. Jihad simply means striving. In this case, it means striving to defend the honour of Muslims and Islam, by going to war as a last resort.

Injuries, death and destruction occur in a war. Therefore, Islam issues fair rules and limits based on Islamic justice. God says:

- "Fight in the cause of God those who fight you, but do not transgress limits, for God loves not transgressors." (2:190)
- "Fight for justice, but if they desist then let there be no hostility." (2:193)

Abdullah Yusuf Ali, in his translation of the Qur'an *The Meaning of the Glorious Qur'an*, says: "War is only permissible in self-defence, and under well-defined limits. In any case, strict limits must not be transgressed: women, children, old and infirm men should not be molested, nor trees and crops cut down, nor peace withheld when the enemy comes to terms."

In a war, Muslims are prohibited from any heartless acts against the enemies. Prophet Muhammad addressed his followers, when they were ready for a battle, with these words: "In fighting back against the injuries inflicted upon us, disturb not the votaries of monastic seclusion, spare the weakness of the female sex, injure not the infant, or those who are ill in bed. Abstain from demolishing the dwellings of the unresisting inhabitants, destroy not the means of their subsistence, nor their fruit trees and touch not the palm."

Abu Bakar, the first Caliph of Islam, in carrying out Islamic justice in a war, instructed the Muslim army thus: "Do not be harsh on them (the enemies); do not kill their children, old men and women; do not cut down or burn palm trees, do not destroy fruit trees, do not slay sheep or camels except for food. If you see people who have taken refuge in a place of worship (of any religion) let them be safe in their place of refuge."

Islam detests aggression, terrorism and destruction, and loves peace and the doing of good. God says: "Strive together (as in a competitive race) towards all that is good."(2:148) & (5:51)

NO IMAGES OF GOD AND PROPHETS
God says that "there is none like Him." (112:4) Since God says that nothing looks like Him, no Muslim painter or sculptor in his right mind would dare diminish God's majesty and magnificence by making Him look like someone or something through a painting or statue.

Prophets are also highly respected. Muslims adore and respect Prophet Muhammad so much that they would not dare belittle him by making images of him that could never truly depict him at any point in his age.

In the Hollywood movie *The Message*, which recounts the endeavours of Prophet Muhammad, the producers were wise in not engaging any actor for the role of the Prophet. The Prophet was not seen in the movie, only his existence was felt. The role of Ali, the Prophet's cousin and son-in-law, was also not acted by anyone. The nearest relative to the Prophet portrayed in the movie was Hamza, the Prophet's uncle, a role acted by veteran Anthony Quinn. The producers had consulted the Al-Azhar University in Cairo on the story for accuracy and the subtleties of Islam. This consultation was certainly a praiseworthy effort as the sensitivities of Muslims were considered.

Prophet Muhammad is one of the most successful personalities in history, having attained the greatest achievements in the history of religions. He was never lost in the labyrinth of myth and mythology. He was the most adored and respected person by billions in Islamic history. This would have easily driven an ignorant, overzealous Muslim to regard him as a god or deity, and worship him! For this very reason, no images of the Prophet are allowed anywhere.

The Prophet himself had prohibited the creation of a replica of him in any form, lest an ignorant Muslim, though out of love and overenthusiasm, frames up a painting of him or places a statue of him in his home and starts to worship him (the created) instead of the Creator.

SUPERSTITIOUS BELIEFS AND PRACTICES

To avoid bad luck, some people say "touch wood" and look around for any wooden material to touch. For example, someone might say, "I was talking to a person who has tuberculosis. I hope I won't contract it, touch wood!"

In fact, across cultures, even among Muslim communities in some countries, people get caught up in irrational acts, like touching wood, crossing fingers, throwing (raw) rice over newlyweds, throwing salt on the path of dear ones who are parting to live somewhere else, circling the head of a sick person with a hard-boiled egg or placing a chilli in the open to stop rain for the day, and so on. They do these things in the belief that they can avoid or prevent anything bad from happening to them. Some of these acts have become part of their cultures.

The fact is, whether one touches wood or not, if a mishap is ordained to happen, it cannot be thwarted. In Islam, such acts intended to reverse bad luck are not miracles but superstition. Islam does not condone superstition. God knows best of what has been "fixed" — bad or good in the reckoning of any individual.

Islam teaches people to trust God. What an individual reckons as bad for him might be good for nature, for other people and for research and knowledge. Muslims who condone superstitious practices and beliefs do so out of ignorance about the true nature of Islam. Islam is rational. The Qur'an teaches Muslims to use their intellect and reason in whatever they do — to believe rationally is the thread that runs through the Qur'an.

During the time of Prophet Muhammad, the majority of the Arabs were steeped in superstition. The Prophet had condemned superstitious beliefs as they go against the Islamic teaching of *Tawakkul* (God's Will).

But, *tawakkul* should not be confused with foresight and planning. *Tawakkul* does not mean that one should sit idly and not make any efforts of his own to plan for the future. Placing chilli to stop rain is not *tawakkul* but superstition; it is not scientific. *Tawakkul* means that any future happening that is ordained to take place will happen and cannot be avoided. Everything goes according to God's Will and Plan. Only God knows the outcome. But the *do'a* (supplication) for good things to happen must go on.

God forbids certain beliefs and activities that could result in harm, danger and corruption, not only to one's self but also to the community. Islam teaches people to "work" and plan for the future in the best of intentions, and place their trust in God. The Qur'an says: "Worship God and put your trust in Him." (11:123)

One of the earliest incidents in the history of Islam that could have become a popular superstition happened when Prophet Muhammad's only son died in infancy. On that day, there was an eclipse of the sun and some people began to say that even the sun mourned the death of the infant. The Prophet quickly pointed out that celestial phenomenon had nothing to do with the affairs of human beings, thus nipping the belief in the bud; otherwise this incident could have well developed into a widespread superstitious belief.

A popular ritual based on superstitious belief that prevailed in Singapore, even up to 1965, was one known as *mandi Safar* (bathing in the Muslim month of Safar). Many Malay and Indian Muslims used to go to the sea in Safar, the second month of the Muslim calendar, to take a dip in the sea. Soaking themselves in the sea, according to their (mistaken) belief, would wash away their sins. Those who were unable to go to the sea bought mango leaves that had Qur'anic verses written on them. They soaked the leaves in pails of water and used the water to bathe. These practices have no basis in Islam. Sins can only be atoned by sincere repentance; it cannot be washed away by mere water. And there is no such thing as holy water in Islam.

Fortune-telling is forbidden, because having knowledge of one's bad future is more distressful or disadvantageous than not knowing it. Black magic is also forbidden, because the services of black magicians involve negative and harmful activities. Whenever such activities are carried out, both the service provider as well as the client become involved in sin. The Prophet said: "To learn black magic or fortune-telling and to practise it is a rejection of the faith of Islam." He also said: "He who goes to a sorcerer or the witch doctor, denies by his action what has been revealed by Islam."

Predictions, say, of natural disasters like earthquakes by seismologists, or of storms by the meteorological department, are however not prohibited because they involve scientific knowledge. Scientific knowledge is never alienated with Islam.

There is also no such thing as bad luck numbers or auspicious dates for weddings or for moving house as all these are superstition. As Muslims become more aware of the teachings of Islam, all ignorantly condoned superstitious beliefs die away.

OFFERINGS AND VISITS TO GRAVES

It is insulting to the majesty of God to offer Him anything, whether blood or food items, to please Him or reward Him for any fortunes, or to offer Him any item when imploring for His help in any misfortune. God, who is Great and Self-sufficient (6:133), does not require offerings of any kind or the sacrifice of an animal for its blood or meat.

Muslims do not worship anything created by human beings; they worship God alone, the Creator. God says: "Those who invoke besides God have nothing (and therefore vain is their worship) as they (idols) are themselves created. They are things dead, lifeless ..." (16:20–21)

It is *haram* (unlawful) to ask for divine favours from anyone dead or alive, saints and pious personalities included, or to seek spiritual favours at the graves of ancestors or at the *keramat* (shrines of saints and pious or important personalities). The departed, however loving, pious or great they were when alive, are in another kind of existence where contact with the worldly existence is impossible. Otherwise all departed parents would not fail to contact their living children to help them.

Islam discourages any idea of mediation, recommendation or intercession by any human being, dead or alive. Instead, it encourages direct contact with God for divine assistance. God says: "Call on Me: I will answer your prayers." (40:60)

It is a virtuous act to visit the graves of pious personalities, ancestors, relatives or friends to offer *do'a*, seeking forgiveness to the dead for any sin they might have committed when they were alive. Except for flowers to adorn the graves, offerings of any kind, including fruits and food, for the dead are strictly prohibited in Islam because the spirit of the dead needs no worldly food to sustain itself.

FLEXIBILITY IN ISLAM

God desires that Muslims practise Islam comfortably with ease. He therefore provides flexibility and allowance for certain Islamic practices during situational emergencies and exigencies of time. God says that He "does not burden anyone beyond his capabilities" (2:286).

Some examples where flexibility can be applied are:

- *Haram* meat: pork is *haram* but in an emergency or when life is threatened, Islam allows pork to be eaten until the emergency ends.
- Ramadan fasting: women who are menstruating and at an advanced stage of pregnancy, the sick and travellers need not fast, but they have to make up for the missed number of days after Ramadan. Those who are infirm (advanced in age) and insane need not repay the missed days. A person who fasts can stop fasting any time if he suddenly feels unwell and needs to take medicine. Also, if he forgetfully eats or drinks, his fast would not be nullified as long as he stops the act immediately upon realising the mistake.
- *Solat*: menstruating women need not perform the *solat*. Unlike the Ramadan fast, they need not repay the missed ones later. Insane people need not be forced to perform the *solat*. A person who, for some reason, is unable to perform the postures required in the *solat* can perform the *solat* in any way convenient to him until he is able to perform it in the normal way. For example, if a man has a knee injury, he can perform his *solat* while sitting on a chair at home or in the mosque. If one is travelling in a foreign country, he can shorten the length of the four-*raka'at* (units) *solat* to just two units, and even perform it in advance or later for some of the *solat*.
- Haj: the Haj is the fifth Pillar of Islam and a Muslim has to undertake the pilgrimage to Mecca at least once in his lifetime. Yet, he need not undertake it if he is poor, infirm or has health problems.

Islam allows flexibility for Islamically accepted reasons. But abuse of the rules is a sin. God advises Muslims that Islamic practices are undertaken for their own good: "Whoever will believe, it is for the good of his own soul." (6:104)

ACCEPTANCE BY OWN PEOPLE

For a universal religion from God, very rightly, the very first people who joined its fold should be those who were near and dear to the person who taught or delivered it — because logically they were the ones who would better understand the character and sincerity of the person preaching it and the authenticity of the teaching itself. It should also be a religion first accepted by his own people and by his own country. Indeed, this happened to Islam.

The very first people who joined the fold of Islam were those who knew Prophet Muhammad best — the Prophet's wife (Khadijah), his relatives (his uncle, Hamza, and his cousin, Ali), and friends (like Abu Bakar). Quite a number of other people of Mecca embraced Islam too.

Very unfortunately, the pagan Arabs in Mecca found Islam to be opposed to their carefree lifestyle, a decadent one, and so mercilessly persecuted the Prophet and his followers. This resulted in the Prophet migrating to Medina (known as Hijrah) where Islam was welcomed. When after 10 years in Medina, the Prophet re-entered Mecca, he harboured no anger, malice or revenge on any of his enemies, not even on his bitterest enemy, Abu Sufiyan. Surprised that no vengeance was taken against him, and after days of careful thought, Abu Sufiyan went to the Prophet and pronounced the *Shahadah*, declaring to become a Muslim. The notable general Khalid ibn Walid, who defeated the Prophet's army in the Battle of Uhud, also embraced Islam. Many others followed suit.

People in the whole of Arabia became Muslims within 30 years of the demise of the Prophet. Today, Islam is the official religion of Saudi Arabia. Some 1.7 billion people of various races and cultures in the world are Muslims.

FREEDOM OF RELIGION

Since the Prophet's time, people have been attracted to Islam because of its uniqueness, beauty, rationality, universality and dynamism.

Another notable characteristic of Islam that makes it attractive to people is the freedom of belief, and this is mentioned in the Qur'an. God says: "There is no compulsion in the faith," because "The right way is clearly distinct from error." (2:256). The Qur'an adds: "If it had been your Lord's Will, they would have believed — all who are on earth!" (10:99) But God did not make every human being a believer without choice. God made man special, endowing him with superior intelligence.

As man can think and make choices, the Prophet was not allowed by God to compel people to become Muslims (10:99). Instead, God commanded the Prophet to call people to Islam with wisdom and kindness. God says: "(O Muhammad!) Invite (people) to the way of your Lord with wisdom and beautiful preaching, and reason with them in ways that are best and most gracious." (16:125)

As Islam is a religion established by the Prophet himself (and not one formulated ages after the founder's death), the Prophet sent letters to rulers of neighbouring countries inviting them to embrace Islam; no one was forced to convert as the Prophet had closely followed the instructions of the Qur'an. Therefore, in the course of his 23 years of Apostolic mission, the Prophet did not compel anyone to accept Islam against his own free will, not even his own uncle and guardian, Abu Talib, who was never formally converted to Islam.

God advised the Prophet to tell those with other religions, thus: "You have your faith and I have my faith." (109:6) However, as a comprehensive and completed Religion of God for mankind, Muslims are requested to pass the Message of Islam to others, believers and non-believers, so that they will not hold Islam in contempt. The Islamic method of Islam-sharing is: "Invite (people) to the way of your Lord with wisdom." (16:125) This is an invitation taught by God Himself. It is a gracious and intellectual way of inviting people to understand Islam — by wisdom.

22 ⬛ THE HEREAFTER

Life on this earth is a test. God says that He tests "you to see which one of you is best in work ..." (67:2) Those who have been righteous on earth would, in the Hereafter, dwell in the "Eternal Home", commonly known as "Paradise". God says: "If any do deeds of righteousness — be they male or female — and have faith, they will enter Paradise, and not the least injustice will be done to them." (4:124)

DEATH
When a person dies, his soul leaves the body to exist in another dimension, commonly referred to as the next world or the Hereafter.

When a Muslim hears of the death of another Muslim, he responds by saying softly, *"Inna lillahi wa inna illaihi raji'un"*. This is a direct quotation from of the Qur'an: "To God we belong and to Him is our return." (2:156) For this reason, death is not unwelcomed and burial is not delayed. The dead is buried as soon as possible, often within 24 hours.

The Muslim funeral is solemn and simple. There are no banners or wreaths. Devotedness is observed, and the funeral rites are carried out inside the home.

There are four basic funeral rituals: cleansing the body, clothing it with seamless white cloth, performing prayers for it and burying it.

The *jenazah* (dead body) is first bathed. A person who is a family member, relative or friend of the same gender may assist the person conducting this ritual.

The body, which should not be preserved by any method or embalming, is then wrapped with a piece of seamless white cotton cloth. In death everybody is equal. A millionaire or a pauper is wrapped similarly. The face is exposed until people have paid their last respects. Those at the funeral, even the immediate family members of the deceased, are discouraged from wailing or crying loudly to make a show. Wet eyes, as a result of sorrow, are natural and normal.

When the family members, relatives and friends have paid their last respects, the *jenazah* is placed in a coffin-like carrier. Muslims do not just leave it to the staff of the casket company to transport the body. Able-bodied male Muslims — family members, relatives, friends, neighbours and even those who do not know the deceased — would eagerly help to carry the *jenazah* from the home to the waiting transport and then to the grave site. Before the burial, people perform the *jenazah solat* (Islamic prayers for the dead). This is usually conducted in the home or at any mosque along the way to the cemetery.

At the cemetery, the body is lifted from the carrier and placed into the grave, the whole body touching the earth and the face facing towards the *qibla* (direction of the Ka'aba in Mecca).

Muslims do not use a coffin to bury the dead. Only an inexpensive, undecorated ordinary wooden box, open at the top and bottom, is used. A loose lid (wooden cover) is placed over the body so as to temporarily protect it from being crushed by the earth when the grave is filled with earth. The idea is to allow the body to touch the earth and be absorbed by it over time.

When the grave is covered with earth, a prayer, called *talqin*, is said at the graveside to conclude the burial service. The *talqin*, apart from beseeching God's blessing for the dead, addresses the listeners, reminding them to be righteous as they too would have to return to God through such a burial.

The grave need not be marked by any strong or expensive structure that would last for ages. A simple and inexpensive structure would do to mark the place for loved ones to offer their *do'a* (supplication). For those unable to visit the grave, the *do'a* can be offered individually every day — after their *solat*. Such regular heartfelt practice after the daily prayers is indeed worthy and noble.

RESURRECTION

Death is a gateway to the spiritual world just like birth is a gateway to this physical world. Nobody can escape death. "Every soul shall have a taste of death ..." (3:185) Death takes place anytime in a person's life, anywhere, and in any way. "No one knows when he will die or what the future will bring forth, nor does any one know in what land he will die." (31:34)

As for the dead, the Qur'an says: "God will raise them up to be returned to Him." (6:36)

People often wonder how a dead person whose body is already decomposed and disintegrated could be brought back to life. The Qur'an points out that when a doubter asks: "Who can give life to dry bones and a decomposed one at that?" (33:78), the answer is: "He (God), who created them for the first time (in the womb of mothers), will give them life again, for He is well-versed in every kind of creation." (36:79) God has "programmed" the process of birth-living-death-resurrection, all very naturally.

Addressing those in doubt about the reality of the Hereafter, God says: "O mankind! If you have doubt about the Resurrection, (consider) that We created you out of dust, then out of sperm, then out of a leech-like clot, then out of a morsel of flesh, partly formed and partly unformed, in order that We may manifest (our Power) to you; and We cause whom We will to rest in the wombs for an appointed term, then We bring you out as babies, then (foster you) that you may reach your age of full strength; and some of you are called to die; and some are sent back to the feeblest old age, so that they know nothing after having known (much)... And verily the Hour will come; There can be no doubt about it, or about (the fact) that God will raise up all who are in the graves." (22:5–7)

The doubter and the wrongdoer would be afraid to die but there is no escape for them. God says: "Wherever you are, death will find you out, even if you are in towers built up strong and high." (4:78)

JUDGEMENT

There is a day in the Hereafter called Judgement Day, when every person will be questioned concerning "his life, how he expended it; his youth, how he used it; his wealth, from where he got it and how he spent it; and his knowledge, how he made use of it" (Hadith).

God has made each person different. People differ in many ways such as in mental and physical abilities, appearance and wealth. As each of these situations is granted by God, each individual is accountable to Him for any of the ways in which he has been preferred over others.

Some are born blind, others have eyesight; some are born into poor families, others into wealthy families. But how they live with what they are given is the test. The Qur'an points these out:

- "(God) has raised some of you in rank above others, that He may try you in what He has given you." (6:165)
- "You shall certainly be tried and tested in your possessions and in your personal selves ..." (3:186)

Muslims believe that when a person dies, his soul will remain in a timeless dimension called the *alam barzakh* to wait for the Judgement. The following Qur'anic verses say that:

- Judgement is inevitable: "And surely Judgement must come." (51:6)
- Every person will be judged accordingly: "... and on the Day of Judgement will you be paid your full recompense ..." (3:185)
- The Judgement will be fair and just: "Then on this day (Day of Judgement), no soul shall be dealt with unjustly in the least; and you shall not be repaid except for that which you did." (36:54)

With words that human beings can understand, God says that on Judgement Day, He will open the record of every person's deeds for review. "On that Day ... anyone who has done an atom's weight of good, see it. And anyone who has done an atom's weight of evil shall see it." (99:6–8) God explains further: "We shall set up scales of justice for the Day of Judgement, so that not a soul will be dealt with unjustly in the least ..." (21:47)

God's justice requires that there should be reward for any good done, and punishment for evil. Since God's mercy and compassion overshadows all, His Judgement will be balanced and fair.

HEAVEN

When a baby develops in the womb of its mother (the confines of the womb is itself a world of its own), there is no way for the baby to understand the vast potentials of the world outside. Yet, the outside world is a reality. In the same way, people in this world cannot fathom the Hereafter. The next world is described in the Qur'an with words which man can relate to, such as "Gardens" for Heaven and "Fire" for Hell.

After the Day of Judgement, those who do not qualify for admission to Heaven will enter Hell. "Those who are rebellious and wicked, their abode will be in the Fire." (32:20) But "(For those who believe and do good), God has prepared Gardens under which rivers flow, to dwell therein forever: that is the Supreme Felicity." (9:100)

Heaven, also termed as Paradise, is a reward for those believers who have done good and who have purified themselves through righteousness. God says that the dwellers of Heaven will be those who "come to Him as believers who have worked righteous deeds, for them are ranks exalted, Gardens of Eternity, beneath which flow rivers: they will dwell therein for aye: such is the reward of those who purify themselves (from evil)." (20:74–76)

The Qur'an uses varied imagery to describe spiritual matters which are all beyond description in words. Therefore, *Jannah* ("Heaven" or "Paradise") can only be expressed by allegory and imagery.

The expression used in the Qur'an for heavenly bliss is "Garden with rivers flowing". God metaphorically describes Heaven as "Gardens" because a garden, especially one that incorporates flowing water like brooks and low waterfall, is a place that is pleasant, relaxing, rejuvenating, peaceful and enduring. God says that the righteous and truthful will dwell in the "Gardens with rivers flowing beneath — their Eternal Home." (5:122)

23 🕌 GOD'S COMPASSION

In Islam, a personal sin can be forgiven by seeking God's forgiveness with sincere repentance. God, in His infinite mercy and compassion for His creatures, forgives a person's personal sins if he repents and mends his ways before he passes away. "O My servants who have transgressed against their souls. Do not despair of the mercy of God: for God forgives all (personal) sins; for He is Oft-forgiving, Most Merciful." (39:53)

FORGIVENESS

Forgiveness is sought both from God and from fellow human beings for any wrongs committed knowingly or unknowingly. A Muslim is encouraged to seek forgiveness from family members, relatives and friends, whether he has committed sins against them or not and whenever they meet. This is accomplished non-verbally with the *salam* any time they happen to meet, and verbally as well, especially during Eid ul-Fitri (Festival of Charity), when for instance, Malay Muslims will add to their *salam* the phrase *"Maaf zahir dan batin"* ("Forgive me both internally and outwardly").

Forgiveness clears one's "defiled" soul to a certain extent, thus increasing the "purity" of his soul. A person's *fitrah* (pure state) therefore lies in his own hands as well as in the supreme compassion of God. The Qur'an says: "Indeed your Lord is quick in punishment, yet He is indeed Oft-forgiving, Most Merciful." (6:165)

The Qur'an teaches Muslims to repent for whatever wrongs they have done and to seek God's forgiveness immediately before it is too late. "Turn you to your Lord (in repentance) and bow to His Will, before the Penalty comes on you; after that you shall not be helped." (39:54)

The Qur'an repeatedly mentions that God is "Oft-forgiving and Most Merciful" towards man. One of the verses goes: "If anyone does evil or wrongs his own soul but afterward seeks God's forgiveness, He will find God Oft-forgiving, Most Merciful." (4:110)

Islam advises people that the moment they realise their mistake, they should be truly sorry and mend their ways. With God, it is the turning of the heart towards Him that is sufficient to receive His forgiveness. God promises:

- "(Those) who have forsaken the domain of evil and are striving hard in God's cause, it is they who are truly believers. Forgiveness of sins awaits them and a most excellent sustenance." (8:74)
- "Verily, if any of you did evil in ignorance, and thereafter repented, and amended (his conduct), lo! God is Oft-forgiving, Most Merciful." (6:54)

Such are the promises of God in Islam, from the One who is so gracious and compassionate towards all who turn to Him.

REWARD

The essence of Islam is serving God, and serving God means doing good for the benefit of humanity. The Qur'an, in a number of verses, informs people that God "loves those who do good" (3:134) and that He rewards them.

An example of a Qur'anic verse that urges the believer to do good to people is: "Serve God ... and do good to parents, kinsfolk, orphans, those in need, neighbours who are near, neighbours who are strangers, the companion by your side, the wayfarer (you meet) ..." (4:36)

God's reward comes in a variety of forms, material and non-material in nature. If one feels happy by doing good, the happiness one gets is a reward by itself. Good health is another reward. A happy family is yet another kind of reward. The person might even be unaware of the reward given to him, even if it happens to be in some material form, accorded in some indirect way.

God's generosity in giving rewards is mentioned in a number of ways. Here are some of them:

- People are rewarded while they are still on this earth: "Good is the reward for those who do good in this world ... those who patiently persevere will truly receive a reward without measure!" (39:10)
- The doers of good will not get anything less: "God will give them their reward according to the best of what they have done." (39:35)
- The more worthy the deed, the larger is the reward: "Those who believe and work righteous deeds for them shall be reward according to the best of their deeds." (29:7)
- The reward will be better than the merits of the deed: "If any does good, the reward to him is better than his deed ..." (28:84)
- Deeds are doubled and rewarded: "God is never unjust in the least degree: If there is any good (done), He doubles it, and gives from His own presence a great reward." (4:40)
- Rewards are multiplied: "God may reward according to the best of their deeds, and add even more for them out of His grace." (24:38)

In urging people to do good, God prompts: "Let there arise out of you a band of people inviting to all that is good, enjoining what is right and forbidding what is wrong: they are the ones to attain felicity." (3:104)

24 ☪ MUSLIM WORLD

There are today many Muslim countries on the globe, so much so that one often hears the term "the Muslim world" in the media. Indonesia, for instance, has the largest Muslim population. Other countries in Asia, such as Afghanistan, Pakistan and Malaysia have a majority Muslim population. The estimated Muslim population today stands at 1.7 billion.

ISLAMIC COUNTRY
There is a difference between an Islamic country and a Muslim country. The adjective "Islamic" refers to a quality that is positive and wholesome.

A Muslim country is one in which the majority of its population comprises Muslims. Islam may or may not be its official religion. An Islamic country has three features:

1. Its population is vastly Muslim.
2. Islam is declared as its official religion in its constitution.
3. The Shari'ah (Islamic Law) is practised. Islamic righteousness, an important aspect of social life, is not a separate feature of an Islamic country as it is one of the main features of the Shari'ah.

To understand the term "Islamic country" better, one needs to understand the significance of the term "Islamic".

Islam is a religion that guides people (who want to be guided) to be righteous. It is an Islamic way of life (Ad-Deen) in its absolute and practical sense; hence it embraces worldly activities, including politics and the sciences. Thus, putting a child to school is Islamic; taking steps to prevent a crime is Islamic; preventing or annihilating terrorism is Islamic; building a safe playground for the neighbourhood children is Islamic. In other words, any act done or carried out for the purpose of preventing anything that is negative or bad and enhancing anything that is positive or good is Islamic. Any Islamic act is a righteous act.

An Islamic country is therefore one that practises righteous acts for the good and betterment of its people and others in the world. Some of the features of an Islamic country include:

- **Spirit of togetherness:** Enhancing tolerance, peace and harmony among its people to achieve togetherness; respecting other religions and allowing the people to practise their respective faiths.
- **Education opportunities:** Ensuring that education, at least primary education, is compulsory for every child; and that both boys and girls have equal opportunities for higher education.
- **Employment opportunities:** Ensuring that efforts are put to eliminate poverty by creating new and relevant jobs to boost the country's progress; and putting general efforts in improving the country's per capita reserves.
- **Housing schemes:** Ensuring that there is a comprehensive housing scheme in place so that people have a roof over their heads, and putting efforts in improving sanitary amenities.
- **Environment and recreational facilities:** Ensuring that the environment is clean and its people practise cleanliness; and providing people with ample recreational facilities and social amenities.
- **Safety and justice:** Cultivating an environment that is crime-free and corruption-free, and ensuring that people have access to justice; and that people, including visitors and tourists, are safe to travel anywhere in the country.
- **Medical facilities:** Ensuring that the people have comprehensive medical coverage; and that there are adequate medical facilities like clinics and hospitals.
- **Traffic and transport system:** Ensuring an efficient traffic and transport system as well as having good and adequate roads and parking lots.

- **Committed government**: That the government is responsible and committed to the affairs of the country, such as efforts in raising the living standards of the people, and quickly acting on matters concerning emergencies like disasters and epidemics.

Indeed the aim of an Islamic country is for its government to run and govern it efficiently through righteousness and thereby achieve peace, progress and prosperity. God says: "Good is the reward for those who do good in this world." (38:10)

SCHOOLS OF THOUGHT

Generally, Muslims form two unofficial groups: Sunnis and Shi'as (often spelt "Shiites" in the English media). However, the difference between them is only political. The groups originated from a central issue of who should succeed as the ruler of the Islamic state after the demise of Prophet Muhammad.

At the time of the Prophet, there were no such groups known as "Sunni" or "Shia"; there were only "Muslims".

When the Prophet passed away in the Muslim year 11 Hijrah (632 CE), the people needed an able leader to lead the fast expanding Muslim community. They selected Abu Bakar, the most respected elderly companion of the Prophet, as the first Caliph (Successor). After the death of Abu Bakar, three others, all companions of the Prophet, succeeded one after another, again by the people's choice. They were Umar, Othman and finally Ali. This group of the Muslim community who maintained that the Caliphs should be appointed through people's choice became known as "People of the Sunnah" or Sunnis.

However, a section of the Muslim community believed that the Caliphs of the Islamic state should not be selected by the people but be automatically appointed from the Prophet's descendants. They felt that Ali, who was the cousin and son-in-law of the Prophet, should have been appointed as the first Caliph without argument or contest. This group of the Muslim community came to be called "Supporters" or Shi'as. The majority of the Iranians are Shi'as.

There are also sects and religious movements within the Sunnis and Shi'as. The four main sects, referred to as "schools of thought", are Shafii, Hambali, Hanafi and Maliki. These schools of thought take the name of their respective teachers who were renowned Islamic personalities. Although these teachers never sought to start a sect, as time passed their followers adhered strictly to their individual teachings. The difference in thought of one sect on a particular matter may be different from the thought of another, but both are valid. It is like looking at a building from different locations — the view from one location is different from the view from another location, but both views are of the same building.

Regardless of the differing views over certain matters, the followers of each sect recognised the followers of the other sects as Muslims. They would not quarrel with each other over their doctrinal differences should they happen to meet at the mosque for the *solat* or at social gatherings. Muslims of all sects even perform the Haj in Mecca together. In fact, no Sunni or Shi'a would refer to himself other than "Muslim".

In Saudi Arabia, an austere form of Islam called Wahabism is practised. It started as a puritan movement that put more emphasis on the fundamentals of Islam, such as the oneness of God. Wahabis call themselves "Muwahidun" (Unitarians). The name "Wahabi" is used by Westerners after the name of the founder Muhammad bin Abdul Wahab.

Another aspect of Islam is Sufism. It is not a sect but an intense form of Islamic practice concerned with the uplifting of the soul by practising virtues like patience, sincerity, humility and love for God. Anyone from any country can be a Sufi.

The most important unifying factor is that the followers of one sect or movement recognise the legitimacy of the other. They believe in the same common fundamentals — belief in One God (Allah), belief in the Qur'an as God's Words, belief in Prophet Muhammad as the final Messenger of God, and belief in the *Sunnah* (tradition of the Prophet).

The existence of these Islamic sects and movements is the result of democracy and freedom in the interpretation of Islamic teachings within the norms of the divine wisdom. It enriches Islamic tradition, practice and intellectualism.

25 ⛪ ISLAMIC DIRECTION

Islam encourages Muslims, both men and women, to pursue education and acquire *taqwa* (God-consciousness and hence obedience to God) so that they can become righteous or "total" Muslims loved by God and fellowmen of all religions. With education, Muslims are better-informed of the correct teachings of Islam, and so practise Islam with understanding. They are tolerant to one and all, Muslims and non-Muslims alike, and work together for the good of everyone in the community, the nation and the world.

ISLAMIC RELIGIOSITY

The increase in religiosity among Muslims is the result of more and more Muslims understanding Islam and gaining worldly knowledge from various sources — through formal education, ad hoc lectures or courses organised by Islamic bodies and mosques, business dealings, travelling, books, personal contacts and the mass media. They become more aware of the beauty and rationality of Islam, and that a "Muslim" is a person who practises Islam as it should be practised — positively — and be righteous and exemplary.

One of the most important "dress" of Islam is *taqwa*. With *taqwa*, a Muslim keeps himself clean and pure bodily, spiritually, in appearance, and in thought and action.

The outer outlook or physical aspect of the person is important in Islam, namely, to be neat and tidy, to dress decently, and to be modest, courteous and friendly as conduct and character are all part of *taqwa*. Thus, nowadays, as a result of increased education, more Muslim women are noticeably adhering to the Islamic dress code. However, it does not mean that the one who wears the scarf and ignores the other aspects of Islamic discipline earns more merit than the woman who does not wear a scarf but dresses modestly and observes all the practices of Islam. God rewards a person accordingly and fairly.

The woman who observes the Islamic dress code earns spiritual merits; therefore, many Muslim women take the option of "covering up" even the head with the scarf (*tudung*) in answer to: Why leave out a little more (uncovered) and gain less spiritual merit!

In Singapore, for instance, certain developments have been noticed in its Muslim community. A few of these developments include the following:

- More Muslims attend religious classes in mosques and lectures by local and foreign Muslim scholars.
- More women, including polytechnic and university students, wear the *tudung* (headscarf) and any normal clothing that covers the whole body with the face and hands below the wrists uncovered in conformity with *hijab* (Islamic attire).
- More young people go to the mosque to perform the *solat* and take part in its Islamic-based educational activities and programmes.
- More Muslims travel (to both Muslim and non-Muslim countries) with the understanding that travelling is education by itself as taught by Islam.
- More Muslims perform the Haj and Umrah.

To Muslims, these developments show that they are on the right path — the Straight Way of Islam. The outcome of Islamic religiosity is positive. Among other factors, it enables Muslims to:

- become true and better Muslims who relate to all human beings, irrespective of race, language or religion.
- be aware that aggression, fanaticism and terrorism are un-Islamic. For instance, suicide bombers and those who engage in terrorist activities that lead to the death of innocent people, do so against the teachings and the spirit of Islam. Islam places great emphasis on righteousness, peace and harmony among all human beings.
- work closely with people of all races and religions to tackle common concerns for the benefit of everyone.

- aspire to achieve their educational and economic goals.
- enhance the spirit of tolerance and fraternity among all people of the world.
- become good and loyal citizens of their countries of residence and useful members of the global society.

Islamic religiosity is an "Islamic development" process. It stresses that Islam is a religion that is progressive and universal, and that Muslims ought to practise Islam in its true spirit — harmoniously and effectively so as to gain maximum benefit from its teachings, both for this world and the Hereafter. The increase in religiosity makes a Muslim a better person, a better citizen and a better resident of the earth.

HEAVENLY BLISS

God, in His Supreme Mercy and Compassion, invites the "believers" to be always in a state of Islam (Supreme Purity and Peace). God says: "O you who believe! Enter into Islam wholeheartedly, and follow not the footsteps of the evil one for he is to you an avowed enemy." (2:208)

In this divine invitation, God addresses only those who "believe", meaning that if one believes in God, then one should embrace Islam wholeheartedly. Two groups of people are addressed in this verse:

1. Believers (in God) who are non-Muslims: They are only invited, not forced to embrace Islam if they have no inclination for it, hence the use of the word "wholeheartedly".
2. Believers who are Muslims: Do all Muslims follow and practise Islam in the way Islam should be followed and practised? If not, then they are also invited to practise Islam "wholeheartedly".

Even for the Muslim believer, God advises him to practise Islam wholeheartedly and "Die not except in a state of Islam" (3:10). For a Muslim to be "in a state of Islam", he must be a "balanced" and "total" Muslim, one who adheres to all Islamic practices such as the *solat*, fasting, charity, strengthening friendship, promoting peace, and refraining from all *haram* activities like gambling, theft, corruption, terrorism, revenge killing and destroying lives and property.

Only such Muslims — those "who believe and do good" (22:23) — are the ones who would enter Heaven. God says: "Verily, God will admit those who believe and do good to the Gardens (Heaven)" (22:23) and again: "Those who repent and believe, and work righteousness will enter the Garden — Gardens of Eternity (Heaven)." (19:60–61)

For the righteous, God promises heavenly bliss with such expressions as:

- "Those who do right and refrain from wrong have a great reward." (3:172)
- "Those who do deeds of righteousness, male or female, and have faith, will enter Heaven." (4:124)
- "Those who come to Him (God) as believers who have worked righteous deeds, for them are ranks exalted — Gardens of Eternity in which they will dwell forever." (20:75–76)

God has shown people the Straight Way (Islam), the Way that provides guidance for the attainment of well-being in this world and spiritual development for the next world. Those who follow the Way shall be admitted to "Gardens of Eternity" and that is the Islamic salvation, "the supreme achievement" (44:57). "Their greeting therein will be: 'Peace!'" (14:23)

🕌 EPILOGUE

The Qur'an urges Muslims to practise Islam correctly and positively according to its guiding principles and to help promote righteousness.

"Those who believe (in the One God) and practise righteousness" (2:25) will go to Jannah (Paradise) — this promise is found throughout the Qur'an. The word "righteousness", appearing 201 times in 193 verses in the Qur'an, refers to Islamic practices of goodness and piety, such as performing the *solat*, fasting, giving of *zakat*, promoting and strengthening of friendship, and refraining from *haram* acts such as theft, corruption, revenge killing, suicide bombings and terrorism.

Islam teaches Muslims never to alienate people of other faiths but to be close to them to promote respect, understanding and harmony. "O mankind, We have created you from a single pair of male and female and made you into nations and tribes that you may know one another (not to despise one another). Indeed, the most noble of you in the sight of God is the most righteous of you." (49:13)

The Islamic faith advises Muslims to live peacefully with all fellow human beings because every human being, Muslim or non-Muslim, is God's creation. God's Mercy extends to all humans and creatures. God says: "My Mercy encompasses all things." (7:156)

The media frequently delivers reports of terrorists — identified as Muslims — killing innocent human beings, both Muslims and non-Muslims. If they were true Muslims and understand Islam to its core, they would not indulge in killings as God has given a stern and weighty warning: "Whoever kills a person ... it is as if he had killed all mankind." (5:32) But, it is most likely that not all acts of terrorism have bearings on Islam but are consequences of the political and social leanings of the perpetrators' countries or sectarian strife, and so are secular in nature, having nothing to do with the faith of the perpetrator.

There are also reports of radicalism of young adults who had gathered their "knowledge" of Islam not from recognised institutions and teachers but from the Internet, only to be led astray. They might follow a so-called religious leader blindly no matter how absurd the teachings. Many such leaders, charismatic in personality and affable in speech, have come in grace and gone in disgrace. It is important for the less religiously informed Muslims to be aware of teachings from such personalities and avoid getting influenced from their rhetoric.

It is also important for non-Muslims not to react emotionally over acts of terrorism committed by so-called Muslims who are few in number as compared to the vast majority of peace-loving Muslims. Terrorists are wayward people whose victims are also Muslims. So, non-Muslims should not bear any hatred or animosity towards all Muslims. Islamophobia is as bad as terrorism and can disunite the society. Both Muslim and non-Muslim security and interfaith officials ought to stand in solidarity and sincerity in tackling terrorism in proper ways together as a harmonious community.

A non-Muslim Singaporean, Mr Tang Li, in his letter to the Forum of *The Straits Times*, 27 June 2017, says: "It is particularly important for Singaporeans to remember that although the terrorist attacks in Manchester and London were committed by people claiming to be fighting for Islam, the Muslims who live in Singapore are people who share the same aspirations for a peaceful life as the rest of us.

"Singapore's Muslim community has been a source of blessing for me. The highlight of my working life was working for the Saudi Embassy. When I was unemployed, it was a Muslim friend who employed me. I know that these (attacks) are not things that the majority of Muslims would ever condone.

"A Muslim taxi driver once told me: 'The first religion of mankind is *Salaam* (Peace) — the action of two different people coming together, to shake hands and be friends.' I have never forgotten these words. I hope all Singaporeans will keep this in mind whenever we read about violent sectarian conflicts in the world."

God advises Muslims to practise Islam wholeheartedly and "Die not except in a state of Islam." (3:102) Abdullah Yusuf Ali, commenting on this verse in *The Meaning of the Glorious Qur'an*, says: "Our whole being should be permeated with Islam; it is not a mere veneer or outward show." Muslims should be "people inviting to all that is good, enjoining what is right, and forbidding what is wrong." (3:104)

 **APPENDICES**

APPENDIX A

Chapters of the Qur'an
The Qur'an comprises 114 chapters, each with a title. The name of each of the chapters in Romanised Arabic and its corresponding interpretation in English are given in the table below.

Chapter No.	Chapter Name in Arabic	Chapter Name in English
01	Al-Fatiha	The Opening (Chapter)
02	Al-Baqarah	The Cow
03	Ali-Imran	The Family of Imran
04	An-Nisaa	The Women
05	Al-Maida	The Table Spread (or The Repast)
06	Al-An'am	The Cattle
07	Al-A'raf	The Heights (or The Faculty of Discernment)
08	Al-Anfal	The Spoils of War
09	At-Tauba	Repentance
10	Yunos	Jonah
11	Hud	Hood

12	Yusof	Joseph
13	Ar-Ra'd	Thunder
14	Ibrahim	Abraham
15	Al-Hijr	The Rocky Tract
16	Al-Nahl	The Bee
17	Al-Isra	The Night Journey
18	Al-Kahf	The Cave
19	Maryam	Mary (mother of Jesus Christ)
20	Ta-Ha	(*Mystic letters*)
21	Al-Anbiya	The Prophets
22	Al-Haj	The Pilgrimage
23	Al-Mu'minun	The Believers
24	An-Nur	The Light
25	Al-Furqan	The Criterion (or The Standard of Truth and False)
26	Ash-Shu'araa	The Poets
27	An-Naml	The Ants
28	Al-Qasas	The Narration
29	Al-Ankabut	The Spider
30	Ar-Rum	The Roman Empire
31	Luqman	Luqman (the wise)
32	As-Sajda	Prostration
33	Al-Ahzab	The Confederates
34	Saba	(The City of) Sheba
35	Al-Fatir	The Originator (of Creation)
36	Ya-Sin	(*Mystic letters*)
37	As-Saffat	Those ranked in ranks
38	Sad	(*Mystic letters*)
39	Az-Zumar	The Crowds

40	Ghafir	Forgiving
41	Fussilat	Clearly Spelt Out
42	Ash-Shura	Consultation
43	Az-Zukhruf	Gold Ornaments
44	Ad-Dukhan	Smoke
45	Al-Jathiya	Kneeling Down
46	Al-Ahqaf	The Sand-Dunes
47	Muhammad	Muhammad
48	Al-Fath	Victory
49	Al-Hujurat	The Private Apartments
50	Qaf	(*Mystic letters*)
51	Az-Zariyat	Dust-Scattering Winds
52	At-Tur	Mount
53	An-Najm	The Stars
54	Al-Qamar	The Moon
55	Ar-Rahman	Most Gracious (God)
56	Al-Waqi'a	The Inevitable (Event)
57	Al-Hadid	Iron
58	Al-Mujadala	The Woman who Pleads
59	Al-Hashr	The Gathering or The Banishment
60	Al-Muntahana	The Examined One
61	As-Saff	Battle Array or The Ranks
62	Al-Jumu'a	The Assembly (for Friday prayers)
63	Al-Munafiqun	The Hypocrites
64	At-Tagabun	Mutual Loss and Gains
65	At-Talaq	Divorce
66	At-Tahrim	Holding (something) to be Forbidden

67	Al-Mulk	Dominion or The Sovereign
68	Al-Qalam	The Pen
69	Al-Haqqa	The Reality
70	Al-Ma'arij	The Ways of Accent
71	Nuh	Noah
72	Al-Jinn	The Spirits
73	Al-Muzzamil	The Enshrouded One
74	Al-Muddath-thir	The Cloaked One
75	Al-Qiyamat	The Resurrection
76	Al-Insan	The Human Beings
77	Al-Mursalat	Those Sent Forth
78	Al-Nabaa	The (Great) News
79	An-Nazi'at	Those Dragged Forth
80	Abasa	He Frowned
81	At-Takwir	The Folding Up
82	Al-Infitar	The Cleaving Asunder
83	Al-Mutafifin	Dealing in Fraud
84	Al-Inshiqaq	The Rending Asunder
85	Al-Buruj	The Great Constellations
86	At-Tariq	The Morning Star
87	Al-A'la	(God) The Most High
88	Al-Gashiya	The Overwhelming (Event)
89	Al-Fajr	The Dawn
90	Al-Balad	The City
91	Al-Shams	The Sun
92	Al-Lail	The Night
93	Ad-Duha	The Glorious Morning Light
94	Ash-Sharh	The Expansion or The Opening-up of the Heart

95	At-Tin	The Fig
96	Iqraa or Al-Alaq	Read ! or The Clot
97	Al-Qadr	The Night of Power or Destiny
98	Al-Baiyina	The Clear Evidence
99	Al-Zilzal	The Earthquake
100	Al-Adiyat	Those who Run
101	Al-Qari'a	The Sudden Calamity
102	At-Takathur	Greed for more and more
103	Al-Asr	The Flight of Time
104	Al-Humaza	The Scandal-monger
105	Al-Fil	The Elephant
106	Quraish	The Quraish (who were the custodians of the Ka'aba)
107	Al-Ma'un	Neighbourly Needs
108	Al-Kauthar	Abundance
109	Al-Kafirun	Those who Deny the Truth
110	An-Nasr	Help
111	Al-Lahab	The Flame
112	Al-Ikhlas	The Purity (of Faith) or Unity (of God)
113	Al-Falaq	The Dawn or Daybreak
114	An-Nas	Mankind

APPENDIX B

Everyday usage of "Allah"

A Muslim celebrates his joy with Allah and praises Him by using His name often and frequently. The following are the various words and phrases with the word "Allah" a Muslim uses or hears often, some even every day.

"Alhamdulillah" (Praise be to Allah): A Muslim uses this phrase to thank Allah for anything good that happens, however small. For example: "I got an increase in my salary, *alhamdulillah*!" or "I have finished my bowl of rice porridge, *alhamdulilah*."

"Allahu-Akbar" (Allah is Great): This phrase is commonly used by Muslims as a peaceful reminder of their Islamic commitment. It is frequently pronounced during any occasion that is meritorious and virtuous, such as at a marriage solemnisation or a conversion to Islam ceremony. One of the most frequent occasions the phrase is used is during the *azan* (call to prayer), which is delivered five times a day, and during the prayer itself, a Muslim says it softly at the start of each of the postures of the prayer.

"Astaghfirullah" (I seek forgiveness from Allah): Here is an example of when this phrase is said: "*Astaghfirullah*! It's almost *Maghrib* now! How could I have forgotten to perform my *Asar solat*?"

In the azan (prayer call): The *azan* one hears from the mosque or over the radio contains the word "Allah" which is vocalised 11 times. A Muslim listening to it responds to each phrase of the *azan* softly, with phrases that contain the word "Allah". The *azan* recites the *Takbir* — "God is Great" — and the *Shahadah* — "There is no god but God (Allah) and Muhammad is the Messenger of God". (See Chapter 6.)

"Bismillah" (In the name of Allah): This is pronounced whenever a Muslim is about to eat or start a journey or begin a task.

"Insha Allah" (Allah Willing): This is a phrase of assurance given in humility. For example, when a Muslim is invited for a birthday party, instead of haughtily saying, "I will attend", he would say, "I will attend, *Insha Allah.*" This is because he may be unable to attend due to unforeseen circumstances, such as a death or a mishap. It is also an acknowledgement that without the Will and Permission of Allah, no plan can materialise.

During the kuthbah (sermon): During the *kuthbah* and during the prayer that comes after the sermon, the word "Allah" is used and heard numerous times.

"Masha Allah" (As Allah has willed): This phrase is used when admiring or praising something or somebody in recognition that all good things come from Allah and are blessings from Him. For example: "*Masha Allah*! What a cute baby!"

"Nauzubillah" (We seek refuge in Allah (from evil)): Muslims use this phrase to protect themselves from evil thoughts or on hearing unIslamic expressions.

Upon news of death: When a Muslim receives news of the death of another Muslim (whether a friend, relative or anyone else), he says under his breath, "*Inna lillahi wa inna illaihi raji'un.*" The phrase, taken from a Qur'anic verse, means "To Allah we belong and to Him is our return." (2:156) The phrase reminds us that a human being is not eternal but Allah is, and that He gives life and takes it away any time He wills.

When reading the Qur'an: When a Muslim reads the Qur'an, whether at home or at the mosque or at a religious event, he or she begins each chapter with the phrase "*Bismillahir Rahmanir Rahim*" which means "In the name of Allah, Most Compassionate, Most Merciful".

When giving the salam: The *salam*, which literally means 'peace', is the universal greeting of Muslims who greet each other with "*Assalamu alaikum wa rahmatullah*" (May the peace and mercy of Allah be with you). The shorter form of the *salam* is simply "*Assalamu alaikum.*" The obligatory reply to this greeting is: "*Wa-alaikum salam wa rahmatullahi wa barakatuh*" (May the peace, mercy and blessings of Allah be with you, too). Regardless of the race or culture a Muslim belongs to, the exact same phrases are offered and replied whenever one Muslim meets another, even though they may be strangers and do not speak the language of the other. This Islamic greeting cuts across all language barriers and is understood universally.

When pronouncing the Shahadah: This is the testimony of faith pronounced by a convert to Islam at the point of his or her conversion. It goes: "*Ash hadu Allah illaha illallah, wa ash hadu anna Muhammadur Rasullullah.*" (I bear witness that there is no god but Allah and Muhammad is His Messenger.) This declaration of faith forms the basis of conviction in Islam.

When perfoming the solat: A Muslim performs his obligatory *solat* (Muslim prayers) five times daily and during each *solat*, he pronounces the word "Allah" several times. The word "Allah" is also recited several times during all non-obligatory *solat*, known as *sunnat solat*, which are performed before and after the obligatory *solat* as well as upon stepping into the mosque as a respect for the place of prayer.

"SubhanAllah" (Glory to Allah): This phrase is often used when praising Allah or exclaiming awe at His attributes.

"Ya, Allah!": A phrase of exclamation, often uttered in a mishap or upon hearing of a mishap. This phrase is also used when calling Allah in an earnest way during a *do'a* (supplication).

When saying the Zikir (praising or remembrance of Allah): Muslims often say the zikir after their daily prayers, with words such as "*SubhanAllah*", *Alhamdullilah*" and "*Allahu-Akbar*", sometimes using Muslim prayer beads to impart tranquillity and peace to the mind and the soul. Allah says in the Qur'an: "O ye who believes, remember Allah very often and glorify Him morning and evening." (33:41-42) and "Behold in the Remembrance of Allah do hearts find satisfaction." (13-28).

APPENDIX C

The Last Sermon of Prophet Muhammad

Prophet Muhammad delivered this sermon in his last pilgrimage on 9 Zulhijjah 10H (9 Zulhijah of the year 10 Hijrah or 633 CE); this last pilgrimage has come to be known in history as the Prophet's Farewell Pilgrimage. At the end of the sermon, the Prophet received the final Revelation from God, which mentions the name of the religion as Islam. (The peak of the annual Haj is on 9 Zulhijjah, called Arafah Day, the day when pilgrims must be present in the plains of Arafah for the *wukuf* (presence or retreat.) After praising and thanking God, Prophet Muhammad said:

"O People, lend me an attentive ear, for I know not whether after this year, I shall ever be amongst you again. Therefore listen to what I am saying to you very carefully and take these words to those who could not be present here today.

Sacred trust: O People, just as you regard this month, this day, this city, as Sacred, so regard the life and property of every Muslim as a sacred trust. Return the goods entrusted to you to their rightful owners. Hurt no one so that no one may hurt you. Remember that you will indeed meet your Lord, and that He will indeed reckon your deeds. Beware of Satan for the safety of your religion. He has lost all hope that he will ever be able to lead you astray in big things, so beware of following him in small things.

Rights of the wife: O People, it is true that you have certain rights with regard to your women, but they also have rights over you. Remember that you have taken them as your wives only under Allah's trust and with His permission. If they abide by your right then to them belongs the right to be fed and clothed in kindness. Do treat your women well and be kind to them for they are your partners and committed helpers. And it is your right that they do not make friends with any one of whom you do not approve, as well as never to be unchaste.

Muslim obligations: O People, listen to me in earnest, worship Allah, perform your *solat*, fast during the month of Ramadan, and give your wealth in *zakat*. Perform the Haj if you can afford to undertake it.

No racial superiority: All mankind is from Adam and Eve. An Arab has no superiority over a non-Arab nor a non-Arab has any superiority over an Arab; also a white has no superiority over a black nor a black has any superiority over a white except by piety and good action. Learn that every Muslim is a brother to every other Muslim and that the Muslims constitute one brotherhood. Nothing shall be legitimate to a Muslim which belongs to a fellow Muslim unless it was given freely and willingly. Do not, therefore, do injustice to yourselves. Remember, one day you will appear before Allah and answer your deeds. So beware, do not stray from the path of righteousness after I am gone.

Follow Qur'an and *Sunnah*: O People, no prophet or apostle will come after me and no new faith will be born. Reason well, therefore, O People, and understand the words which I convey to you. I leave behind two things, the Qur'an and my example, the *Sunnah*, and if you follow these you will never go astray. All those who listen to me shall pass my words to others and those to others again; and may the last ones understand my words better than those who listen to me directly. Be my witness, O Allah, that I have conveyed your Message to your people".

Final Revelation from God: "This day, I have perfected your religion for you, and have completed My favour upon you; and have chosen for you Islam as your religion." (5:4)

A few months after delivering the sermon, Prophet Muhammad passed away in Medina and was buried in the simple house where he lived. Today, this burial site is situated in Masjidil Nabawi (the Prophet's Mosque). Pilgrims to Mecca for the Haj or Umrah would not fail to take the opportunity to go to Medina to perform the solat *in this huge mosque and pay a visit to the Prophet's grave to offer* do'a *(blessings) to him.*

The tomb is enclosed in a chamber with small grilled windows. Against the walls of the chamber, uniformed staff stand on guard to keep order in the area and to prevent overwhelmed pilgrims from staying too long offering supplications.

APPENDIX D

The Islamic Prayers (Solat)

The names of the five *solat* and the starting time for each of the *solat* for 31 January, 10 May and 22 September 2016 in Singapore are given as a sample for comparison in the table below:

	Solat	Period	Raka'at (Units)	31 Jan 2016 (hrs)	10 May 2016 (hrs)	22 Sep 2016 (hrs)
1	Suboh	just-after dawn *solat*	2	0556	0536	0538
2	Zohor	early afternoon *solat*	4	1320	1303	1259
3	Asar	late afternoon *solat*	4	1641	1624	1600
4	Maghrib	just-after dusk *solat*	3	1920	1907	1901
5	Ishak	night *solat*	4	2033	2019	2010

The time (in 24 hours) shows the entry time of each of the *solat* for 31 January, 10 May and 22 September as indicated in the *solat* timetable of 2016 in Singapore. The timetable, printed in a card form, is given away free-of-charge by Muslim organisations. It is also printed on the calendar and in the Malay/Muslim newspapers.

APPENDIX E

Difference between *solat* and *do'a* (supplication)

Solat	Do'a
Performed at fixed periods of the day and night	Sought or said any time, but also good to say it immediately after the *solat*
Ablution is obligatory	Not necessary, but preferable
Face towards the Ka'aba	Not necessary, but preferable
Various postures necessary, if possible	No postures necessary, except raised open palms, if possible
Said in Arabic	Said in Arabic and own language, or any language the supplicant is comfortable with
For own benefit	For own benefit as well as for others, the community and country

APPENDIX F

The Hijrah calendar
The months of the Hijrah calendar, showing a few main events of Islam:

No.	Name of the months	Main events on the Hijrah calendar
1	Muharram	1 Muharram: Zikral Hijrah or Muslim New Year
2	Safar	
3	Rabiul Awal	12 Rabiul Awal: Maulidur Rasul or Birthday of Prophet Muhammad
4	Rabiul Akhir	
5	Jamadil Awal	
6	Jamadil Akhir	
7	Rejab	27 Rejab: Isra'-Mi'raj or the Ascension of Prophet Muhammad to Heaven, also known as the Night Journey of the Prophet
8	Sha'aban	
9	Ramadan	(a) 1 Ramadan: commencement of the month-long Ramadan fast; (b) 17 Ramadan: Nuzul Al-Qur'an or Commemoration of the commencement of the Revelations of the Qur'an
10	Shawal	1 Shawal: Eid ul-Fitri (Festival of Charity), commonly called Hari Raya Aidil Fitri, a term sometimes spelt in one word, Aidilfitri, in Malay
11	Zulkaedah	
12	Zulhijjah	10 Zulhijjah: Eid ul-Adha (Festival of Sacrifice), commonly called Hari Raya Haji in Malay

ABOUT THE AUTHOR

Shaik Kadir holds a Master in Education degree from the University of Sheffield, UK. He received training in teaching and journalism both locally and overseas, and has years of experience as an educator and journalist. Formerly a senior lecturer at the Institute of Technical Education, Singapore, he has now retired from service.

His numerous writings have been published in many magazines in Singapore and in other countries. Many of his articles have also appeared in local newspapers such as *The Straits Times* and *Berita Harian*.

Kadir is the author of several books, one of which was an autobiographical novel, *A Kite in the Evening Sky*, first published in 1989 and the revised edition in 2000.

He has written several books on aspects of Islam. These include: *Read! The Islamic Inspiration on Guidance, Wisdom and Progress* (1986), *The Straight Way: Answers and Questions Put Forward by Non-Muslims* (1993), *The Haj: The Annual Pilgrimage of Islam* (1995), *Commanding a Dynamic Islamic Personality* (2000), *Inside Islam: 101 Questions and Answers* (2004), *Islam Explained* (2006) which has been translated into Malay with the title *Pendekatan Islam* (2009), *Allah: Understanding God in Islam* (2016) and *Splendours of Islam: More than 100 Common Questions about Islam* (2007) which went into a second edition in 2016.